DEFINITIONS
FIRST SERIES

DEFINITIONS
FIRST SERIES

★

Essays in Contemporary Criticism by
HENRY SEIDEL CANBY, Ph.D.
Lecturer in English at Yale University

KENNIKAT PRESS, INC./PORT WASHINGTON, N. Y.

ACKNOWLEDGMENTS

THE author wishes to acknowledge the courtesy of *The Atlantic Monthly, Harper's Magazine, The Century Magazine, The Literary Review* of *The New York Evening Post, The Bookman, The Nation,* and *The North American Review* for permission to reprint such of these essays as have appeared in their columns.

PREFACE

THE unity of this book is to be sought in the point of view of the writer rather than in a sequence of chapters developing a single theme and arriving at categorical conclusions. Literature in a civilization like ours, which is trying to be both sophisticated and democratic at the same moment of time, has so many sources and so many manifestations, is so much involved with our social background, and is so much a question of life as well as of art, that many doors have to be opened before one begins to approach an understanding. The method of informal definition which I have followed in all these essays is an attempt to open doors through which both writer and reader may enter into a better comprehension of what novelists, poets, and critics have done or are trying to accomplish. More than an entrance upon many a vexed controversy and hidden meaning I cannot expect to have achieved in this book; but where the door would not swing wide I have at least tried to put one foot in the crack. The sympathetic reader may find his own way further; or may be stirred by my endeavor to a deeper appreciation, interest, and insight. That is my hope.

New York, April, 1922.

CONTENTS

PREFACE

I. ON FICTION

II. ON THE AMERICAN TRADITION

III. THE NEW GENERATION

IV. THE REVIEWING OF BOOKS

V. PHILISTINES AND DILETTANTE

VI. MEN AND THEIR BOOKS

CONCLUSION

I
On Fiction

Sentimental America

THE Oriental may be inscrutable, but he is no more puzzling than the average American. We admit that we are hard, keen, practical,—the adjectives that every casual European applies to us,—and yet any book-store window or railway news-stand will show that we prefer sentimental magazines and books. Why should a hard race—if we are hard—read soft books?

By soft books, by sentimental books, I do not mean only the kind of literature best described by the word "squashy." I doubt whether we write or read more novels and short stories of the tear-dripped or hyper-emotional variety than other nations. Germany is—or was—full of such soft stuff. It is highly popular in France, although the excellent taste of French criticism keeps it in check. Italian popular literature exudes sentiment; and the sale of "squashy" fiction in England is said to be threatened only by an occasional importation of an American "best-seller." We have no bad eminence here. Sentimentalists with enlarged hearts are international in habitat, although, it must be admitted, especially popular in America.

When a critic, after a course in American novels and magazines, declares that life, as it appears on the printed page here, is fundamentally sentimental-ized, he goes much deeper than "mushiness" with his

3

charge. He means, I think, that there is an alarming
tendency in American fiction to dodge the facts of
life—or to pervert them. He means that in most popular books only red-blooded, optimistic people are welcome. He means that material success, physical soundness, and the gratification of the emotions have the
right of way. He means that men and women (except
the comic figures) shall be presented, not as they are,
but as we should like to have them, according to a
judgment tempered by nothing more searching than
our experience with an unusually comfortable, safe, and
prosperous mode of living. Every one succeeds in
American plays and stories—if not by good thinking,
why then by good looks or good luck. A curious society
the research student of a later date might make of it—
an upper world of the colorless successful, illustrated
by chance-saved collar advertisements and magazine
covers; an underworld of grotesque scamps, clowns,
and hyphenates drawn from the comic supplement; and
all—red-blooded hero and modern gargoyle alike—
always in good humor.

I am not touching in this picture merely to attack
it. It has been abundantly attacked; what it needs
is definition. For there is much in this bourgeois,
good-humored American literature of ours which rings
true, which is as honest an expression of our individuality as was the more austere product of ante-
bellum New England. If American sentimentality does
invite criticism, American sentiment deserves defense.

Sentiment—the response of the emotions to the ap-

peal of human nature—is cheap, but so are many other
good things. The best of the ancients were rich in it.
Homer's chieftains wept easily. So did Shakespeare's
heroes. Adam and Eve shed "some natural tears"
when they left the Paradise which Milton imagined
for them. A heart accessible to pathos, to natural
beauty, to religion, was a chief requisite for the pro-
tagonist of Victorian literature. Even Becky Sharp
was touched—once—by Amelia's moving distress.

Americans, to be sure, do not weep easily; but if they
make equivalent responses to sentiment, that should
not be held against them. If we like "sweet" stories,
or "strong"—which means emotional—stories, our
taste is not thereby proved to be hopeless, or our
national character bad. It is better to be creatures
of even sentimental sentiment with the author of
"The Rosary," than to see the world *only* as it is
portrayed by the pens of Bernard Shaw and Anatole
France. The first is deplorable; the second is dangerous. I should deeply regret the day when a simple
story of honest American manhood winning a million
and a sparkling, piquant sweetheart lost all power to
lull my critical faculty and warm my heart. I doubt
whether any literature has ever had too much of honest
sentiment.

Good Heavens! Because some among us insist that
the mystic rose of the emotions shall be painted a
brighter pink than nature allows, are the rest to forego
glamour? Or because, to view the matter differently,
psychology has shown what happens in the brain when

a man falls in love, and anthropology has traced marriage to a care for property rights, are we to suspect the idyllic in literature wherever we find it? Life is full of the idyllic; and no anthropologist will ever persuade the reasonably romantic youth that the sweet and chivalrous passion which leads him to mingle reverence with desire for the object of his affections, is nothing but an idealized property sense. Origins explain very little, after all. The bilious critics of sentiment in literature have not even honest science behind them.

I have no quarrel with traffickers in simple emotion —with such writers as James Lane Allen and James Whitcomb Riley, for example. But the average American is not content with such sentiment as theirs. He wishes a more intoxicating brew, he desires to be persuaded that, once you step beyond your own experience, feeling rules the world. He wishes—I judge by what he reads—to make sentiment at least ninety per cent efficient, even if a dream-America, superficially resemblant to the real, but far different in tone, must be created by the obedient writer in order to satisfy him. His sentiment has frequently to be sentimentalized before he will pay for it. And to this fault, which he shares with other modern races, he adds the other heinous sin of sentimentalism, the refusal to face the facts.

This sentimentalizing of reality is far more dangerous than the romantic sentimentalizing of the "squashy" variety. It is to be found in sex-stories which carefully observe decency of word and deed, where the

conclusion is always in accord with conventional morality, yet whose characters are clearly immoral, indecent, and would so display themselves if the tale were
truly told. It is to be found in stories of "big business"
where trickery and rascality are made virtuous at the
end by sentimental baptism. If I choose for the hero
of my novel a director in an American trust; if I make
him an accomplice in certain acts of ruthless economic
tyranny; if I make it clear that at first he is merely
subservient to a stronger will; and that the acts he
approves are in complete disaccord with his private
moral code—why then, if the facts should be dragged
to the light, if he is made to realize the exact nature
of his career, how can I end my story? It is evident
that my hero possesses little insight and less firmness
of character. He is not a hero; he is merely a tool.
In, let us say, eight cases out of ten, his curve is already
plotted. It leads downward—not necessarily along the
villain's path, but toward moral insignificance.

And yet, I cannot end my story that way for Americans. There *must* be a grand moral revolt. There
must be resistance, triumph, and not only spiritual, but
also financial recovery. And this, likewise, is sentimentality. Even Booth Tarkington, in his excellent
"Turmoil," had to dodge the logical issue of his story;
had to make his hero exchange a practical literary idealism for a very impractical, even though a commercial,
utopianism, in order to emerge apparently successful
at the end of the book. A story such as the Danish
Nexö's "Pelle the Conqueror," where pathos and the

idyllic, each intense, each beautiful, are made convincing by an undeviating truth to experience, would seem to be almost impossible of production just now in America.

It is not enough to rail at this false fiction. The chief duty of criticism is to explain. The best corrective of bad writing is a knowledge of why it is bad. We get the fiction we deserve, precisely as we get the government we deserve—or perhaps, in each case, a little better. Why are we sentimental? When that question is answered, it is easier to understand the defects and the virtues of American fiction. And the answer lies in the traditional American philosophy of life.

To say that the American is an idealist is to commit a thoroughgoing platitude. Like most platitudes, the statement is annoying because from one point of view it is indisputably just, while from another it does not seem to fit the facts. With regard to our tradition, it is indisputable. Of the immigrants who since the seventeenth century have been pouring into this continent a proportion large in number, larger still in influence, has been possessed of motives which in part at least were idealistic. If it was not the desire for religious freedom that urged them, it was the desire for personal freedom; if not political liberty, why then economic liberty (for this too is idealism), and the opportunity to raise the standard of life. And of course all these motives were strongest in that earlier immigration which has done most to fix the state of mind and body which we call being American. I need not labor the argument. Our political and social history support it; our best literature demonstrates it, for no men have been more idealistic than the American writers whom we have consented to call great. Emerson, Thoreau, Hawthorne, Whitman—was idealism ever more thoroughly incarnate than in them?

And this idealism—to risk again a platitude—has been in the air of America. It has permeated our religious sects, and created several of them. It has given tone to our thinking, and even more to our feeling. I do not say that it has always, or even usually, determined our actions, although the Civil War is proof of its power. Again and again it has gone aground roughly when the ideal met a condition of living—a fact that will provide the explanation for which I seek. But optimism, "boosting," muck-raking (not all of its manifestations are pretty), social service, religious, municipal, democratic reform, indeed the "uplift" generally, is evidence of the vigor, the bumptiousness of the inherited American tendency to pursue the ideal. No one can doubt that in 1918 we believed, at least, in idealism.

Nevertheless, so far as the average individual is concerned, with just his share and no more of the race-tendency, this idealism has been suppressed, and in some measure perverted. It is this which explains, I think, American sentimentalism.

Consider, for example, the ethics of conventional American society. The American ethical tradition is perfectly definite and tremendously powerful. It belongs, furthermore, to a population far larger than the "old American" stock, for it has been laboriously inculcated in our schools and churches, and impressively driven home by newspaper, magazine, and book. I shall not presume to analyze it save where it touches literature. There it maintains a definite attitude toward all sex-problems: the Victorian, which is not necessarily, or even probably, a bad one. Man should be chaste, and proud of his chastity. Woman must be so. It is the ethical duty of the American to hate, or at least to despise, all deviations, and to pretend—for the greater prestige of the law—that such sinning is exceptional, at least in America. And this is the public morality he believes in, whatever may be his private experience in actual living. In business, it is the ethical tradition of the American, inherited from a rigorous Protestant morality, to be square, to play the game without trickery, to fight hard but never meanly. Over-reaching is justifiable when the other fellow has equal opportunities to be "smart"; lying, tyranny—never. And though the opposites of all these laudable practices come to pass, he must frown on them in public, deny their rightness even to the last cock-crow —especially in the public press.

American political history is a long record of idealistic tendencies toward democracy working painfully through a net of graft, pettiness, sectionalism, and bravado, with constant disappointment for the idealist who believes, traditionally, in the intelligence of the crowd. American social history is a glaring instance of how the theory of equal dignity for all men can entangle itself with caste distinctions, snobbery, and the power of wealth. American economic history betrays the pioneer helping to kick down the ladder which he himself had raised toward equal opportunity for all. American literary history—especially contemporary literary history—reflects the result of all this for the American mind. The sentimental in our literature is a direct consequence.

The disease is easily acquired. Mr. Smith, a broker, finds himself in an environment of "schemes" and "deals" in which the quality of mercy is strained, and the wind is decidedly not tempered to the shorn lamb. After all, business is business. He shrugs his shoulders and takes his part. But his unexpended fund of native idealism—if, as is most probable, he has his share—seeks its due satisfaction. He cannot use it in business; so he takes it out in a novel or a play where, quite contrary to his observed experience, ordinary people like himself act nobly, with a success that is all the more agreeable for being unexpected. His wife, a woman with strange stirrings about her heart, with motions toward beauty, and desires for a significant life and rich, satisfying experience, exists in day-long pettiness, gossips, frivols, scolds, with money enough to do what she pleases, and nothing vital to do. She also relieves her pent-up idealism in plays or books— in high-wrought, "strong" novels, not in adventures in society such as the kitchen admires, but in stories with violent moral and emotional crises, whose characters, no matter how unlifelike, have "strong" thoughts, and make vital decisions; succeed or fail significantly. Her brother, the head of a wholesale dry-goods firm, listens to the stories the drummers bring home of night life on the road, laughs, says to himself regretfully that the world has to be like that; and then, in logical reaction, demands purity and nothing but aggressive purity in the books of the public library.

The hard man goes in for philanthropy (never before so frequently as in America); the one-time "boss" takes to picture-collecting; the railroad wrecker gathers rare editions of the Bible; and tens of thousands of humbler Americans carry their inherited idealism into the necessarily sordid experiences of life in an imperfectly organized country, suppress it for fear of being thought "cranky" or "soft," and then, in their imagination and all that feeds their imagination, give it vent. You may watch the process any evening at the "movies" or the melodrama, on the trolley-car or in the easy chair at home.

This philosophy of living which I have called American idealism is in its own nature sound, as is proved in a hundred directions where it has had full play. Suppressed idealism, like any other suppressed desire, becomes unsound. And here lies the ultimate cause of the taste for sentimentalism in the American *bourgeoisie*. An undue insistence upon happy endings, regardless of the premises of the story, and a craving for optimism everywhere, anyhow, are sure signs of a "morbid complex," and to be compared with some justice to the craving for drugs in an alcoholic deprived of liquor. No one can doubt the effect of the suppression by the Puritan discipline of that instinctive love of pleasure and liberal experience common to us all. Its unhealthy reaction is visible in every old American community. No one who faces the facts can deny the result of the suppression by commercial, bourgeois, prosperous America of our native idealism. The student of society may find its dire effects in politics, in religion, and in social intercourse. The critic cannot overlook them in literature; for it is in the realm of the imagination that idealism, direct or perverted, does its best or its worst.

Sentiment is not perverted idealism. Sentiment *is* idealism, of a mild and not too masculine variety. If it has sins, they are sins of omission, not commission. Our fondness for sentiment proves that our idealism, if a little loose in the waist-band and puffy in the cheeks, is still hearty, still capable of active mobilization, like those comfortable French husbands whose plump and smiling faces, careless of glory, careless of everything but thrift and good living, one used to see figured on a page whose superscription read, "Dead on the field of honor."

The novels, the plays, the short stories, of sentiment may prefer sweetness, perhaps, to truth, the feminine to the masculine virtues, but we waste ammunition in attacking them. There never was, I suppose, a great literature of sentiment, for not even "The Sentimental Journey" is truly great. But no one can make a diet exclusively of "noble" literature; the charming has its own cozy corner across from the tragic (and a much bigger corner at that). Our uncounted amorists of tail-piece song and illustrated story provide the readiest means of escape from the somewhat uninspiring life that most men and women are living just now in America.

The sentimental, however,—whether because of an excess of sentiment softening into "slush," or of a morbid optimism, or of a weak-eyed distortion of the facts of life,—is perverted. It needs to be cured, and its cure is more truth. But this cure, I very much fear, is not entirely, or even chiefly, in the power of the "regular practitioner," the honest writer. He can be honest; but if he is much more honest than his readers, they will not read him. As Professor Lounsbury once said, a language grows corrupt only when its speakers grow corrupt, and mends, strengthens, and becomes pure with them. So with literature. We shall have less sentimentality in American literature when our accumulated store of idealism disappears in a laxer generation; or when it finds due vent in a more responsible, less narrow, less monotonously prosperous life than is lived by the average reader of fiction in America. I would rather see our literary taste damned forever than have the first alternative become—as it has not yet—a fact. The second, in these years rests upon the knees of the gods.

All this must not be taken in too absolute a sense. There are medicines, and good ones, in the hands of writers and of critics, to abate, if not to heal, this plague of sentimentalism. I have stated ultimate causes only. They are enough to keep the mass of Americans reading sentimentalized fiction until some fundamental change has come, not strong enough to hold back the van of American writing, which is steadily moving toward restraint, sanity, and truth. Every honest composition is a step forward in the cause; and every clear-minded criticism.

But one must doubt the efficacy, and one must doubt the healthiness, of reaction into cynicism and sophisticated cleverness. There are curious signs, especially in what we may call the literature of New York, of a growing sophistication that sneers at sentiment and the sentimental alike. "Magazines of cleverness" have this for their keynote, although as yet the satire is not always well aimed. There are abundant signs that the generation just coming forward will rejoice in such a pose. It is observable now in the colleges, where the young literati turn up their noses at everything American,—magazines, best-sellers, or one-hundred-night plays,—and resort for inspiration to the English school of anti-Victorians: to Remy de Gourmont, to Anatole France. Their pose is not altogether to be blamed, and the men to whom they resort are models of much that is admirable; but there is little promise for American literature in exotic imitation. To see ourselves prevailingly as others see us may be good for modesty, but does not lead to a self-confident native art. And it is a dangerous way for Americans to travel. We cannot afford such sophistication yet. The English wits experimented with cynicism in the court of Charles II, laughed at blundering Puritan morality, laughed at country manners, and were whiffed away because the ideals they laughed at were better than their own. Idealism is not funny, however censurable its excesses. As a race we have too much sentiment to be frightened out of the sentimental by a blasé cynicism.

At first glance the flood of moral literature now upon us—social-conscience stories, scientific plays, platitudinous "moralities" that tell us how to live—may seem to be another protest against sentimentalism. And that the French and English examples have been so warmly welcomed here may seem another indication of a reaction on our part. I refer especially to "hard" stories, full of vengeful wrath, full of warnings for the race that dodges the facts of life. H. G. Wells is the great exemplar, with his sociological studies wrapped in description and tied with a plot. In a sense, such stories are certainly to be regarded as a protest against truth-dodging, against cheap optimism, against "slacking," whether in literature or in life. But it would be equally just to call them another result of suppressed idealism, and to regard their popularity in America as proof of the argument which I have advanced in this essay. Excessively didactic literature is often a little unhealthy. In fresh periods, when life runs strong and both ideals and passions find ready issue into life, literature has no burdensome moral to carry. It digests its moral. Homer digested his morals. They transfuse his epics. So did Shakespeare.

Not so with the writers of the social-conscience school. They are in a rage over wicked, wasteful man. Their novels are bursted notebooks—sometimes neat and orderly notebooks, like Mr. Galsworthy's or our own Ernest Poole's, sometimes haphazard ones, like those of Mr. Wells, but always explosive with reform. These gentlemen know very well what they are about, especially Mr. Wells, the lesser artist, perhaps, as compared with Galsworthy, but the shrewder and possibly the greater man. The very sentimentalists, who go to novels to exercise the idealism which they cannot use in life, will read these unsentimental stories, although their lazy impulses would never spur them on toward any truth not sweetened by a tale.

And yet, one feels that the social attack might have been more convincing if free from its compulsory service to fiction; that these novels and plays might have been better literature if the authors did not study life in order that they might be better able to preach. Wells and Galsworthy also have suffered from suppressed idealism, although it would be unfair to say that perversion was the result. So have our muckrakers, who, very characteristically, exhibit the disorder in a more complex and a much more serious form, since to a distortion of facts they have often enough added hypocrisy and commercialism. It is part of the price we pay for being sentimental.

If I am correct in my analysis, we are suffering here in America, not from a plague of bad taste merely, nor only from a lack of real education among our myriads of readers, nor from decadence—least of all, this last. It is a disease of our own particular virtue which has infected us—idealism, suppressed and perverted. A less commercial, more responsible America, perhaps a less prosperous and more spiritual America, will hold fast to its sentiment, but be weaned from its sentimentality.

Free Fiction

WHAT impresses me most in the contemporary short story as I find it in American magazines, is its curious sophistication. Its bloom is gone. I have read through dozens of periodicals without finding one with fresh feeling and the easy touch of the writer who writes because his story urges him. And when with relief I do encounter a narrative that is not conventional in 'structure and mechanical in its effects, the name of the author is almost invariably that of a newcomer, or of one of our few uncorrupted masters of the art. Still more remarkable, the good short stories that I meet with in my reading are the trivial ones,—the sketchy, the anecdotal, the merely adventurous or merely picturesque; as they mount toward literature they seem to increase in artificiality and constraint; when they propose to interpret life they become machines, and nothing more, for the discharge of sensation, sentiment, or romance. And this is true, so far as I can discover, of the stories which most critics and more editors believe to be successful, the stories which are most characteristic of magazine narrative and of the output of American fiction in our times.

I can take my text from any magazine, from the most literary to the least. In the stories selected by all of them I find the resemblances greater than the differences, and the latter seldom amount to more than a greater or a less excellence of workmanship and style. The "literary" magazines, it is true, more frequently surprise one by a story told with original and consummate art; but then the "popular" magazines balance this merit by their more frequent escape from mere prettiness. In both kinds, the majority of the stories come from the same mill, even though the minds that shape them may differ in refinement and in taste. Their range is narrow, and, what is more damning, their art seems constantly to verge upon artificiality.

These made-to-order stories (and this is certainly not too strong a term for the majority of them) are not interesting to a critical reader. He sticks to the novel, or, more frequently, goes to France, to Russia, or to England for his fiction, as the sales-list of any progressive publisher will show. And I do not believe that they are deeply interesting to an uncritical reader. He reads them to pass the time; and, to judge from the magazines themselves, gives his more serious attention to the "write-ups" of politics, current events, new discoveries, and men in the public eye,—to reality, in other words, written as if it were fiction, and more interesting than the fiction that accompanies it, because, in spite of its enlivening garb, it is guaranteed by writer and editor to be true. I am not impressed by the perfervid letters published by the editor in praise of somebody's story as a "soul-cure," or the greatest of the decade. They were written, I suppose, but they are not typical. They do not insult the intelligence as do the ridiculous puffs which it is now the fashion to place like a sickly lime-light at the head of a story; but they do not convince me of the story's success with the public. Actually, men and women, discussing these magazines, seldom speak of the stories. They have been interested,—in a measure. The "formula," as I shall show later, is bound to get that result. But they have dismissed the characters and forgotten the plots.

I do not deny that this supposedly successful short story is easy to read. It is—fatally easy. And here precisely is the trouble. To borrow a term from dramatic criticism, it is "well made," and that is what makes it so thin, so bloodless, and so unprofitable to remember, in spite of its easy narrative and its "punch." Its success as literature, curiously enough for a new literature and a new race like ours, is limited, not by crudity, or inexpressiveness, but by form, by the very rigidity of its carefully perfected form. Like other patent medicines, it is constructed by formula.

It is not difficult to construct an outline of the "formula" by which thousands of current narratives are being whipped into shape. Indeed, by turning to the nearest textbook on "Selling the Short Story," I could find one ready-made. (There could be no clearer symptom of the disease I wish to diagnose than these many "practical" textbooks, with their over-emphasis upon technique and their under-estimate of all else that makes literature.) The story *must* begin, it appears, with action or with dialogue. A mother packs

her son's trunk while she gives him unheeded advice
mingled with questions about shirts and socks; a corrupt and infuriated director pounds on the mahogany
table at his board meeting, and curses the honest fool
(hero of the story) who has got in his way; or,
" 'Where did Mary Worden get that curious gown?' in-
quired Mrs. Van Deming, glancing across the sparkling
glass and silver of the hotel terrace." Any one of these
will serve as instance of the break-neck beginning which
Kipling made obligatory. Once started, the narrative
must move, move, move furiously, each action and
every speech pointing directly toward the unknown
climax. A pause is a confession of weakness. This
Poe taught for a special kind of story; and this a later
generation, with a servility which would have amazed
that sturdy fighter, requires of all narrative. Then
the climax, which must neatly, quickly, and definitely
end the action for all time, either by a solution you have
been urged to hope for by the wily author in every pre-
ceding paragraph, or in a way which is logically correct but never, never suspected. O. Henry is responsible for the vogue of the latter of these two alterna-
tives,—and the strain of living up to his inventiveness
has been frightful. Finally comes a last suspiration,
usually in the advertising pages. Sometimes it is a
beautiful descriptive sentence charged with sentiment,
sometimes a smart epigram, according to the style of
story, or the "line" expected of the author. Try this,
as the advertisements say, on your favorite magazine.

This formula, with variations which readers can supply for themselves or draw from textbooks on the short story, is not a wholly bad method of writing fiction. It is, I venture to assert, a very good one,—if you desire merely effective story-telling. It is probably the best way of making the short story a thoroughly efficient tool for the presentation of modern life. And there lies, I believe, the whole trouble. The short story, its course plotted and its form prescribed, has become too efficient. Now efficiency is all that we ask of a railroad, efficiency is half at least of what we ask of journalism; but efficiency is not the most, it is perhaps the least, important among the undoubted elements of good literature.

In order to make the short story efficient, the dialogue, the setting, the plot, the character development, have been squeezed and whittled and moulded until the means of telling the story fit the ends of the story-telling as neatly as hook fits eye. As one writer on how to manufacture short stories tells us in discussing character development, the aspirant must—

"Eliminate every trait or deed which does not help peculiarly to make the character's part in the particular story either intelligible or open to such sympathy as it merits;

"Paint in only the 'high lights,' that is . . . never qualify or elaborate a trait or episode, merely for the sake of preserving the effect of the character's full reality."

And thus the story is to be subdued to the service of the climax as the body of man to his brain.

But what these writers upon the short story do not tell us is that efficiency of this order works backward as well as forward. If means are to correspond with ends, why then ends must be adjusted to means. Not only must the devices of the story-teller be directed with sincerity toward the tremendous effect he wishes to make with his climax upon you and me, his readers; but the interesting life which it is or should be his purpose to write about for our delectation must be manœuvered, or must be chosen or rejected, not according to the limitation which small space imposes, but with its suitability to the "formula" in mind. In brief, if we are to have complete efficiency, the right kind of life and no other must be put into the short-story hopper. Nothing which cannot be told rapidly must be dropped in, lest it clog the smoothly spinning wheels. If it is a story of slowly developing incongruity in married life, the action must be speeded beyond probability, like a film in the moving pictures, before it is ready to be made into a short story. If it is a tale of disillusionment on a prairie farm, with the world and life flattening out together, some sharp climax must be provided nevertheless, because that is the only way in which to tell a story. Indeed it is easy to see the dangers which arise from sacrificing truth to a formula in the interests of efficiency.

This is the limitation by form; the limitation by subject is quite as annoying. American writers from Poe down have been fertile in plots. Especially since O. Henry took the place of Kipling as a literary mas-

ter, ingenuity, inventiveness, cleverness in its American
sense, have been squandered upon the short story. But
plots do not make variety. Themes make variety.
Human nature regarded in its multitudinous phases
makes variety. There are only a few themes in current
American short stories,—the sentimental theme from
which breed ten thousand narratives; the theme of intellectual analysis and of moral psychology favored by
the "literary" magazines; the "big-business" theme;
the theme of American effrontery; the social-contrast
theme; the theme of successful crime. Add a few
more, and you will have them all. Read a hundred examples, and you will see how infallibly the authors—
always excepting our few masters—limit themselves to
conventional aspects of even these conventional themes.
Reflect, and you will see how the first—the theme of
sentiment—has overflowed its banks and washed over
all the rest, so that, whatever else a story may be, it
must somewhere, somehow, make the honest American
heart beat more softly.

There is an obvious cause for this in the taste of the
American public, which I do not propose to neglect.
But here too we are in the grip of the "formula," of
the idea that there is only one way to construct a short
story—a swift succession of climaxes rising precipi-
tously to a giddy eminence. For the formula is rigid,
not plastic as life is plastic. It fails to grasp innumerable stories which break the surface of American life
day by day and disappear uncaught. Stories of quiet
homely life, events significant for themselves that never

reach a burning climax, situations that end in irony, or doubt, or aspiration, it mars in the telling. The method which makes story-telling easy, itself limits our variety.

Nothing brings home the artificiality and the narrowness of this American fiction so clearly as a comparison, for better and for worse, with the Russian short story. I have in mind the works of Anton Tchekoff, whose short stories have now been translated into excellent English. Fresh from a reading of these books, one feels, it is true, quite as inclined to criticize as to praise. Why are the characters therein depicted so persistently disagreeable, even in the lighter stories? Why are the women always freckled, the men predominantly red and watery in the eye? Why is the country so flat, so foggy, so desolate; and why are the peasants so lumpish and miserable? Russia before the Revolution could not have been so dreary as this; the prevailing grimness must be due to some mental obfuscation of her writers. I do not refer to the gloomy, powerful realism of the stories of hopeless misery. There, if one criticizes, it must be only the advisability of the choice of such subjects. One does not doubt the truth of the picture. I mean the needless dinginess of much of Russian fiction, and of many of these powerful short stories.

Nevertheless, when one has said his worst, and particularly when he has eliminated the dingier stories of the collection, he returns with an admiration, almost passionate, to the truth, the variety, above all to the freedom of these stories. I do not know Russia or the Russians, and yet I am as sure of the absolute truth of that unfortunate doctor in "La Cigale," who builds up his heroic life of self-sacrifice while his wife seeks selfishly elsewhere for a hero, as I am convinced of the essential unreality, except in dialect and manners, of the detectives, the "dope-fiends," the hard business men, the heroic boys and lovely girls that people most American short stories. As for variety,—the Russian does not handle numerous themes. He is obsessed with the dreariness of life, and his obsession is only occasionally lifted; he has no room to wander widely through human nature. And yet his work gives an impression of variety that the American magazine never attains. He is free to be various. When the mood of gloom is off him, he experiments at will, and often with consummate success. He seems to be sublimely unconscious that readers are supposed to like only a few kinds of stories; and as unaware of the taboo upon religious or reflective narrative as of the prohibition upon the ugly in fiction. As life in any manifestation becomes interesting in his eyes, his pen moves freely. And so he makes life interesting in many varieties, even when his Russian prepossessions lead him far away from our Western moods.

Freedom. That is the word here, and also in his method of telling these stories. No one seems to have said to Tchekoff, "Your stories must move, move, move." Sometimes, indeed, he pauses outright, as life pauses; sometimes he seems to turn aside, as life turns aside before its progress is resumed. No one has ever made clear to him that every word from the first of the story must point unerringly toward the solution and the effect of the plot. His paragraphs spring from the characters and the situation. They are led on to the climax by the story itself. They do not drag the panting reader down a rapid action, to fling him breathless upon the "I told you so" of a conclusion prepared in advance.

I have in mind especially a story of Tchekoff's called "The Night Before Easter." It is a very interesting story; it is a very admirable story, conveying in a few pages much of Russian spirituality and more of universal human nature; but I believe that all, or nearly all, of our American magazines would refuse it; not because it lacks picturesqueness, or narrative suspense, or vivid characterization—all of these it has in large measure. They would reject it because it does not seem to move rapidly, or because it lacks a vigorous climax. The Goltva swollen in flood lies under the Easter stars. As the monk Jerome ferries the traveler over to where fire and cannon-shot and rocket announce the rising of Christ to the riotous monastery, he asks, "Can you tell me, kind master, why it is that even in the presence of great happiness a man cannot forget his grief?" Deacon Nicholas is dead, who alone in the monastery could write prayers that touched the heart. And of them all, only Jerome read his "akaphists." "He used to open the door of his cell and make me sit by him, and we used to read. . . . His face was compassionate and tender—" In the monastery the countryside is crowding to hear the Easter service. The choir sings "Lift up thine eyes, O Zion, and behold." But Nicholas is dead, and there is none to penetrate the meaning of the Easter canon, except Jerome who toils all night on the ferry because they had forgotten him. In the morning, the traveler recrosses the Goltva. Jerome is still on the ferry. He rests his dim, timid eyes upon them all, and then fixes his gaze on the rosy face of a merchant's wife. There is little of the man in that long gaze. He is seeking in the woman's face the sweet and gentle features of his lost friend.

The American editor refuses such a story. There is no plot here, he says, and no "punch." He is wrong, although an imperfect abstract like mine cannot convict him. For the narrative presents an unforgettable portrait of wistful hero-worship, set in the dim mists of a Russian river against the barbaric splendor of an Easter midnight mass. To force a climax upon this poignant story would be to spoil it. And when it appears, as it will, in reprint, in some periodical anthology of current fiction, it will not fail to impress American readers.

But the American editor must have a climax which drives home what he thinks the public wants. If it is not true, so much the worse for truth. If it falsifies the story, well, a lying story with a "punch" is better than a true one that lacks a fire-spitting climax. The audience which judge a play by the effect of its "curtain," will not complain of a trifling illogicality in narrative, or a little juggling with what might happen if the story were life. Of what the editor wants I find a typical example in a recent number of a popular magazine. The story is well written; it is interesting until it begins to lie; moreover it is "featured" as one of the best short stories of the year. An American girl, brought up in luxury, has fed her heart with romantic sentiment. The world is a Christmas tree. If you are good and pretty and "nice," you have only to wait until you get big enough to shake it, and then down will come some present—respect from one's friends and family, perhaps a lover. And then she wakes up. Her father points out that she is pinching him by her extravagance. Nobody seems to want her kind of "niceness"; which indeed does no one much good. There is nothing that she can do that is useful in the world, for she has never learned. She begins to doubt the Christmas tree. There enters a man—a young electrical engineer, highly trained, highly ambitious, but caught in the wheels of a great corporation where he is merely a cog; wanting to live, wanting to love, wanting to be married, yet condemned to labor for many years more upon a salary which perhaps would little more than pay for her clothes. By an ingenious device they are thrown together in a bit of wild country near town, and are made to exchange confidences. So far, no one can complain of the truth of this story; and furthermore it is well told. Here are two products of our social machine, both true to type. Suppose they want to marry? What can we do about it? The story-teller has posed his question with a force not to be denied.

But I wish we had had a Tchekoff to answer it. As for this author, he leads his characters to a conveniently deserted house, lights a fire on the hearth, sets water boiling for tea, and in a few pages of charming romance would persuade us that with a few economies in this rural residence, true love may have its course and a successful marriage crown the morning's adventure. Thus in one dazzling sweep, the greatest and most sugary plum of all drops from the very tip of the Christmas tree into the lap of the lady, who had just learned that happiness in the real world comes in no such haphazard and undeserved a fashion. Really! have we degenerated from Lincoln's day? Is it easy now to fool all of us all of the time, so that a tale-teller dares to expose silly romance at the beginning of his story, and yet dose us with it at the end? Not that one objects to romance. It is as necessary as food, and almost as valuable. But romance that pretends to be realism, realism that fizzles out into sentimental romance—is there any excuse for that? Even if it provides "heart interest" and an effective climax?

The truth is, of course, that the Russian stories are based upon life; the typical stories of the American magazines, for all their realistic details, are too often studied, not from American life but from literary convention. Even when their substance is fresh, their unfoldings and above all their solutions are second-hand. If the Russian authors could write American stories I believe that their work would be more truly popular than what we are now getting. They would be free to be interesting in any direction and by any method. The writer of the American short story is not free.

I should like to leave the subject here with a comparison that any reader can make for himself. But American pride recalls the past glory of our short story, and common knowledge indicates the present reality of a few authors—several of them women—who are writing fiction of which any race might be proud. The optimist cannot resist meditating on the way out for our enslaved short story.

The ultimate responsibility for its present position must fall, I suppose, upon our American taste, which, when taken by and large, is unquestionably crude, easily satisfied, and not sensitive to good things. American taste does not rebel against the "formula." If interest is pricked it does not inquire too curiously into the nature of the goad. American taste is partial to sentiment, and antagonistic to themes that fail to present the American in the light of optimistic romance. But our defects in taste are slowly but certainly being remedied. The schools are at work upon them; journalism, for all its noisy vulgarity, is at work upon them. Our taste in art, our taste in poetry, our taste in architecture, our taste in music go up, as our taste in magazine fiction seems to go down.

But what are the writers of short stories and what are the editors and publishers doing to help taste improve itself until, as Henry James says, it acquires a keener relish than ever before?

It profits nothing to attack the American writer. He does, it may fairly be assumed, what he can, and I do not wish to discuss here the responsibility of the public for his deficiencies. The editor and the publisher, however, stand in a somewhat different relationship to the American short story. They may assert with much justice that they are public servants merely; nevertheless they *do* control the organs of literary expression, and it is through them that any positive influence on the side of restriction or proscription must be exerted, whatever may be its ultimate source. If a lack of freedom in method and in choice of subject is one reason for the sophistication of our short story, then the editorial policy of American magazines is a legitimate field for speculation.

I can reason only from the evidence of the product and the testimony of authors, successful and unsuccessful. Yet one conclusion springs to the eye, and is enough in itself to justify investigation. The critical basis upon which the American editor professes to build his magazine is of doubtful validity. I believe that it is unsound. His policy, as stated in "editorial announcements" and confirmed by his advertisements of the material he selects, is first to find out what the public wants, and next to supply it. This is reasonable in appearance. It would seem to be good commercially, and, as a policy, I should consider it good for art, which must consult the popular taste or lose its vitality. But a pitfall lies between this theory of editorial selection and its successful practice. The editor must really know what the public wants. If he does not, he becomes a dogmatic critic of a very dangerous school.

Those who know the theater and its playwrights, are agreed that the dramatic manager, at least in America, is a very poor judge of what the public desires. The percentage of bad guesses in every metropolitan season is said to be very high. Is the editor more competent? It would seem that he is, to judge from the stability of our popular magazines. But that he follows the public taste with any certainty of judgment is rendered unlikely, not only by inherent improbability, but also by three specific facts: the tiresome succession of like stories which follow unendingly in the wake of every popular success; the palpable fear of the editor to attempt innovation, experiment, or leadership; and the general complaint against "magazine stories." In truth, the American editor plays safe, constantly and from conviction; and playing safe in the short story means the adoption of the "formula," which is sure to be somewhat successful; it means restriction to a few safe themes. He swings from the detective story to the tale of the alien, from the "heart-interest" story to the narrative of "big business." When, as has happened recently, a magazine experimented with eroticism, and found it successful, the initiative of its editor was felt to be worthy of general remark.

If one reduces this imperfect sketch of existing conditions to terms of literary criticism, the result is interesting. There are two great schools of criticism: the judicial and the impressionistic. The judicial critic —a Boileau, a Matthew Arnold—bases his criticism upon fundamental principles. The impressionistic critic follows the now hackneyed advice of Anatole France, to let his soul adventure among masterpieces, and seeks the reaction for good or bad of a given work upon his own finely strung mind. The first group must be sure of the breadth, the soundness, and the just application of their principles. The second group must depend upon their own good taste.

The American editor has flung aside as archaic the fundamental principles of criticism upon which judicial critics have based their opinions. And yet he has chosen to be dogmatic. He has transformed his guess as to what the public wants into a fundamental principle, and acted upon it with the confidence of an Aristotle. He asserts freely and frankly that, in his private capacity, such and such a story pleases *him*, is *good* (privately he is an impressionist and holds opinions far more valid than his editorial judgment, since they are founded upon taste and not upon intuition merely); but that "the public will not like it," or "in our rivalry with seventy other magazines we cannot afford to print this excellent work." He is frequently right. He is also frequently wrong.

I speak not from personal experience, since other reasons in my own case have usually, though not always, led me to agree with the editor's verdict, when it has been unfavorable; but from the broader testimony of many writers, the indisputable evidence of works thus rejected which have later attained success, and the failure of American short fiction to impress permanently the reading public. Based upon an intuition of the public mind, changing with the wind,— always after, never before it,—such editorial judgment, indeed, must be of doubtful validity; must lead in many instances to unwise and unprofitable restrictions upon originality in fiction.

I am well aware that it is useless to consider current American literature without regard to the multitude of readers who, being, like all multitude, mediocre, demand the mediocre in literature. And I know that it is equally foolish to neglect the popular elements in the developing American genius—that genius which is so colloquial now, and yet so inventive; so vulgar sometimes, and yet, when sophistication is not forced upon it, so fresh. I have no wish to evade the necessity for consulting the wishes and the taste of the public, which good sense and commercial necessity alike impose upon the editor. I would not have the American editor less practical, less sensitive to the popular wave; I would have him more so. But I would have him less dogmatic. All forms of dogmatism are dangerous for men whose business it is to publish, not to criticize, contemporary literature. But an unsound and arbitrary dogmatism is the worst. If the editor is to give the people what they want instead of what they have wanted, he must have more confidence in himself, and more belief in their capacity for liking the good. He should be dogmatic only where he can be sure. Elsewhere let him follow the method of science, and experiment. He should trust to his taste in practice as well as in private theory, and let the results of such criticism sometimes, at least, dominate his choice.

In both our "popular" and our "literary" magazines, freer fiction would follow upon better criticism. The readers of the "literary" magazines are already seeking foreign-made narratives, and neglecting the American short story built for them according to the standardized model. The readers of the "popular" magazines want chiefly journalism (an utterly different thing from literature); and that they are getting in good measure in the non-fiction and part-fiction sections of the magazines. But they also seek, as all men seek, some literature. If, instead of imposing the "formula" (which is, after all, a journalistic mechanism—and a good one—adapted for speedy and evanescent effects), if, instead of imposing the "formula" upon all the subjects they propose to have turned into fiction, the editors of these magazines should also experiment, should release some subjects from the tyranny of the "formula," and admit others which its cult has kept out, the result might be surprising. It is true that the masses have no taste for literature,— as a steady diet; it is still more certain that not even the most mediocre of multitudes can be permanently hoodwinked by formula.

But the magazines can take care of themselves; it is the short story in which I am chiefly interested. Better criticism and greater freedom for fiction might vitalize our overabundant, unoriginal, unreal, unversatile,—everything but unformed short story. Its artifice might again become art. Even the more careful, the more artistic work leaves one with the impression that these stories have sought a "line," and found an acceptable formula. And when one thinks of the multitudinous situations, impressions, incidents in this fascinating whirl of modern life, incapable perhaps of presentation in a novel because of their very impermanence, admirably adapted to the short story because of their vividness and their deep if narrow significance, the voice of protest must go up against any artificial, arbitrary limitations upon the art. Freedom to make his appeal to the public with any subject not morbid or indecent, is all the writer can ask. Freedom to publish sometimes what the editor likes and the public may like, instead of what the editor approves because the public has liked it, is all that he needs. There is plenty of blood in the American short story yet, though I have read through whole magazines without finding a drop of it.

When we give literature in America the same opportunity to invent, to experiment, that we have already given journalism, there will be more legitimate successors to Irving, to Hawthorne, to Poe and Bret Harte. There will be more writers, like O. Henry, who write stories to please themselves, and thus please the majority. There will be fewer writers, like O. Henry, who stop short of the final touch of perfection because

American taste (and the American editor) puts no premium upon artistic work. There will be fewer stories, I trust, where sentiment is no longer a part, but the whole of life. Most of all, form, *the* form, the *formula*, will relax its grip upon the short story, will cease its endless tapping upon the door of interest, and its smug content when some underling (while the brain sleeps) answers its stereotyped appeal. And we may get more narratives like Mrs. Wharton's "Ethan Frome," to make us feel that now as much as ever there is literary genius waiting in America.

A Certain Condescension Toward Fiction

I_F only the reader of novels would say what he thinks about fiction! If only the dead hand of hereditary opinion did not grasp and distort what he feels! But he exercises a judgment that is not independent. Books, like persons, he estimates as much by the traditional reputation of the families they happen to be born in as by the merits they may themselves possess, and the traditional reputation of the novel in English has been bad.

Poetry has a most respectable tradition. Even now, when the realistic capering of free verse has emboldened the ordinary man to speak his mind freely, a reviewer hesitates to apply even to bad poetry so undignified a word as trash. The essay family is equally respectable, to be noticed, when noticed at all, with some of the reverence due to an ancient and dignified art. The sermon family, still numerous to a degree incredible to those who do not study the lists of new books, is so eminently respectable that few dare to abuse even its most futile members. But the novel was given a bad name in its youth that has overshadowed its successful maturity.

Our ancestors are much to blame. For centuries they held the novel suspect as a kind of bastard literature, probably immoral, and certainly dangerous to intellectual health. But they are no more deeply responsible for our suppressed contempt of fiction than weak-kneed novelists who for many generations have striven to persuade the English reader that a good story was really a sermon, or a lecture on ethics, or a tract on economics or moral psychology, in disguise. Bernard Shaw, in his prefaces to the fiction that he succeeds in making dramatic, is carrying on a tradition that Chaucer practised before him:

> And ye that holden this tale a folye,—
> As of a fox, or of a cok and hen,—
> Taketh the moralite, good men.

And that was the way they went at it for centuries, always pretending, always driven to pretend, that a good story was not good enough to be worth telling for itself alone, but must convey a moral or a satire or an awful lesson, or anything that might separate it from the "just fiction" that only the immoral and the frivolous among their contemporaries read or wrote. Today we pay the price.

William Painter, her Majesty Queen Elizabeth's clerk of ordnance in the Tower, is an excellent instance. Stricken by a moral panic, he advertised that from his delectable "Palace of Pleasure" the young might "learne how to avoyde the ruine, overthrow, inconvenience and displeasure, that lascivious desire and wanton evil doth bring to their suters and pursuers"—a disingenuous sop to the Puritans. His contemporary,

Geoffrey Fenton, who also turned to story-making, opines that in histories "the dignitye of vertue and fowelenes of vice appereth muche more lyvelye then in any morall teachynge," although he knew that his "histories" were the sheerest, if not the purest, of fiction, with any moral purpose that might exist chiefly of his own creating. A century and more later Eliza Haywood, the ambiguous author of many ambiguous novels of the eighteenth century, prefaces her "Life's Progress Through the Passions" (an ambiguous title) with like hypocrisy: "I am enemy to all romances, novels, and whatever carries the air of them. . . . It is a *real,* not a *fictitious* character I am about to present"—which is merely another instance of fiction disguising itself, this time, I regret to say, as immorality in real life. And so they all go, forever implying that fiction is frivolous or immoral or worthless, until it is not surprising that, as Mr. Bradsher has reminded us, the elder Timothy Dwight of Yale College was able to assert, "Between the Bible and novels there is a gulf fixed which few novel-readers are willing to pass." Richardson was forced to defend himself, so was Sterne, so was Fielding, so was Goldsmith. Dr. Johnson was evidently making concessions when he advised romances as reading for youth. Jeffrey, the critic and tyrant of the next century, summed it all up when he wrote that novels are "generally regarded as among the lower productions of our literature." And this is the reputation that the novel family has brought with it even down to our day.

The nineteenth century was worse, if anything, than earlier periods, for it furthered what might be called the evangelistic slant toward novel-reading, the attitude that neatly classified this form of self-indulgence with dancing, card-playing, hard drinking, and loose living of every description. It is true that the intellectuals and worldly folk in general did not share this prejudice. Walter Scott had made novel-reading common among the well-read; but the narrower sectarians in England, the people of the back country and the small towns in America, learned to regard the novel as unprofitable, if not positively leading toward ungodliness, and their unnumbered descendants make up the vast army of uncritical readers for which Grub Street strives and sweats to-day. They no longer abstain and condemn; instead, they patronize and distrust.

All this—and far more, for I have merely sketched in a long and painful history—is the background seldom remembered when we wonder at the easy condescension of the American toward his innumerable novels.

The fact of his condescension is not so well recognized as it deserves to be. Indeed, condescension may not seem to be an appropriate term for the passionate devouring of romance that one can see going on any day in the trolley-cars, or the tense seriousness with which some readers regard certain novelists whose pages have a message for the world. True, the term will not stretch thus far. But it is condescension that has made the trouble, as I shall try to prove; for all of us, even the tense ones, do patronize that creative instinct playing upon life as it is which in all times and everywhere is the very essence of fiction.

How absurd that here in America we should condescend toward our fiction! How ridiculous in a country even yet so weak and poor and crude in the arts, which has contributed so little to the world's store of all that makes fine living for the mind! What a laughable parallel of the cock and the gem he found and left upon the dung-heap, if we could be proved not to be proud of American fiction! For if the novel and the short story should be left out of America's slender contribution to world literature, the offering would be a small one. Some poetry of Whitman's and of Poe's, some essays of Emerson, a little Thoreau, and what important besides? Hawthorne would be left from the count, the best exemplar of the fine art of moral narrative in any language; Henry James would be left out, the master of them all in psychological character analysis; Poe the story-teller would be missing, and the art of the modern short story, which in English stems from him; Cooper would be lost from our accounting, for all his crudities the best historical novelist after Scott; Mark Twain, Howells, Bret Harte, Irving! The attempt to exalt American literature is grateful if one begins upon fiction.

And how absurd to patronize, to treat with indifferent superiority just because they are members of the novel family, books such as these men have left us, books such as both men and women are writing in

America to-day! Is there finer workmanship in American painting or American music or American architecture than can be found in American novels by the reader willing to search and discriminate? A contemporary poet confessed that he would have rather written a certain sonnet (which accompanied the confession) than have built Brooklyn Bridge. One may doubt the special case, yet uphold the principle. Because a novel is meant to give pleasure, because it deals with imagination rather than with facts and appeals to the generality rather than to the merely literary man or the specialist, because, in short, a novel is a novel, and a modern American novel, is no excuse for priggish reserves in our praise or blame. If there is anything worth criticizing in contemporary American literature it is our fiction.

Absurd as it may seem in theory, we have patronized and do patronize our novels, even the best of them, following too surely, though with a bias of our own, the Anglo-Saxon prejudice traditional to the race. And if the curious frame of mind that many reserve for fiction be analyzed and blame distributed, there will be a multitude of readers, learned and unlearned, proud and humble, critical and uncritical, who must admit their share. Nevertheless, the righteous wrath inspired by the situation shall not draw us into that dangerous and humorless thing, a general indictment. There are readers aplenty who, to quote Painter once more, find their novels "pleasant to avoyde the griefe of a Winters night and length of Sommers day," and are duly

appreciative of that service. With such honest, if un-
exacting, readers I have no quarrel; nor with many
more critical who respect, while they criticize, the art
of fiction. But with the scholars who slight fiction, the
critics who play with it, the general reader who likes
it contemptuously, and the social enthusiast who
neglects its better for its worser part, the issue is direct.
All are the victims of hereditary opinion; but some
should know better than to be thus beguiled.

The Brahman among American readers of fiction is
of course the college professor of English. His attitude (I speak of the type; there are individual variations of note) toward the novel is curious and interesting. It is exhibited perhaps in the title by which such
courses in the novel as the college permits are usually
listed. "Prose fiction" seems to be the favorite description, a label designed to recall the existence of an undeniably respectable fiction in verse that may justify
a study of the baser prose. By such means is so dubi-
ous a term as novel or short story kept out of the
college catalogue!

Yet even more curious is the academic attitude
toward the novel itself. Whether the normal professor
reads many or few is not the question, nor even how
much he enjoys or dislikes them. It is what he permits
himself to say that is significant. Behind every assent
to excellence one feels a reservation: yes, it is good
enough for a novel! Behind every criticism of un-
truth, of bad workmanship, of mediocrity (alas! so
often deserved in America!) is a sneering implication:

but, after all, it is only a novel. Not thus does he treat the stodgy play in stodgier verse, the merits of which, after all, may amount to this, that in appearance it is literary; not thus the critical essay or investigation that too often is like the parasite whose sustaining life comes from the greater life on which it feeds. In the eyes of such a critic the author of an indifferent essay upon Poe has more distinguished himself than if he had written a better than indifferent short story. Fiction, he feels, is the plaything of the populace. The novel is "among the lower productions of our literature." It is plebeian, it is successful, it is multitudinous; the Greeks in their best period did not practise it (but here he may be wrong); any one can read it; let us keep it down, brethren, while we may. Many not professors so phrase their inmost thoughts of fiction and the novel.

And in all this the college professor is profoundly justified by tradition, if not always by common sense. To him belongs that custody of the classical in literature which his profession inherited from the monasteries, and more remotely from the rhetoricians of Rome. And there is small place for fiction, and none at all for the novel and the short story as we know them, in what has been preserved of classic literature. The early Renaissance, with its Sidney for spokesman, attacked the rising Elizabethan drama because it was unclassical. The later Renaissance, by the pen of Addison (who would have made an admirable college professor), sneered at pure fiction, directly and by implication, because it was unclassical. To-day we have lost our veneration for Latin and Greek as languages, we no longer deprecate an English work because it happens to be in English; nevertheless the tradition still grips us, especially if we happen to be Brahmanic. Our college professors, and many less excusable, still doubt the artistic validity of work in a form never dignified by the practice of the ancients, never hallowed, like much of English literature besides, by a long line of native productions adapting classic forms to new ages and a new speech. The epic, the lyric, the pastoral, the comedy, the tragedy, the elegy, the satire, the myth, even the fable, have been classic, have usually been literature. But the novel has never been a preserve for the learned, although it came perilously near to that fate in the days of Shakespeare; has ever been written for cash or for popular success rather than for scholarly reputation; has never been studied for grammar, for style, for its "beauties"; has since its genesis spawned into millions that no man can classify, and produced a hundred thousand pages of mediocrity for one masterpiece. All this (and in addition prejudices unexpressed and a residuum of hereditary bias) lies behind the failure of most professors of English to give the good modern novel its due. Their obstinacy is unfortunate; for, if they praised at all, they would not, like many hurried reviewers, praise the worst best.

I will not say that more harm has been done to the cause of the novel in America by feeble reviewing than by any other circumstance, for that would not be true;

bad reading has been more responsible for the light estimation in which our novel is held. Nevertheless it is certain that the ill effects of a doubtful literary reputation are more sadly displayed in current criticism of the novel than elsewhere. An enormous effusion of writing about novels, especially in the daily papers, most of it casual and conventional, much of it with neither discrimination nor constraint, drowns the few manful voices raised to a pitch of honest concern. The criticism of fiction, taken by and large, is not so good as the criticism of our acted drama, not so good as our musical criticism, not so good as current reviewing of poetry and of published plays.

Are reviewers bewildered by the coveys of novels that wing into editorial offices by every mail? Is the reviewing of novels left to the novice as a mere rhetorical exercise in which, a subject being afforded, he can practise the display of words? Or is it because a novel is only a novel, only so many, many novels, for which the same hurried criticism must do, whether they be bad or mediocre or best? The reviewing page of the standard newspaper fills me with unutterable depression. There seem to be so many stories about which the same things can be said. There seems to be so much fiction that is "workmanlike," that is "fascinating," that "nobly grasps contemporary America," that will "become a part of permanent literature," that "lays bare the burning heart of the race." Of course the need of the journalist to make everything "strong" is behind much of this mockery; but not all. Heredi-

tary disrespect for fiction has more to do with this flood
of bad criticism than appears at first sight.

Far more depressing, however, is the rarity of real
criticism of the novel anywhere. As Henry James, one
of the few great critics who have been willing to take
the novel seriously, remarked in a now famous essay,
the most notable thing about the modern novel in English is its appearance of never having been criticized
at all. A paragraph or so under "novels of the day" is
all the novelist may expect until he is famous, and more
in quantity, but not much more in quality, then. As
for critical essays devoted to his work, discriminating
studies that pick out the few good books from the many
bad, how few they are (and how welcome, now that they
are increasing in number), how deplorably few in comparison with the quantity of novels, in comparison with
the quality of the best novels!

And what of the general public, that last arbiter in
a democracy, whose referendum, for a year at least,
confirms or renders null and void all critical legislation
good or bad? The general public is apparently on the
side of the novelist; to borrow a slang term expressive
here, it is "crazy" about fiction. It reads so much fiction that hundreds of magazines and dozens of publishers live by nothing else. It reads so much fiction
that public libraries have to bait their serious books
with novels in order to get them read. It is so avid for
fiction that the trades whose business it is to cultivate
public favor, journalism and advertising, use almost
as much fiction as the novel itself. A news article or

an interview or a Sunday write-up nowadays has character, background, and a plot precisely like a short
story. Its climax is carefully prepared for in the best
manner of Edgar Allan Poe, and truth is rigorously
subordinated (I do not say eliminated) in the interest
of a vivid impression. Advertising has become half
narrative and half familiar dialogue. Household goods
are sold by anecdotes, ready-made clothes figure in epi-
sodes illustrated by short-story artists, and novelettes,
distributed free, conduct us through an interesting fiction to the grand climax, where all plot complexities
are untangled by the installation of an automatic water-
heater. I am not criticizing the tendency—it has made
the pursuit of material comfort easier and more interesting,—but what a light it throws upon our mania for
reading stories!

Alas! the novel needs protection from its friends.
This vast appetite for fiction is highly uncritical. It
will swallow anything that interests, regardless of the
make-up of the dish. Only the inexperienced think
that it is easy to write an interesting story; but it is
evident that if a writer can be interesting he may lack
every other virtue and yet succeed. He can be a bad
workman, he can be untrue, he can be sentimental, he
can be salacious, and yet succeed.

No one need excite himself over this circumstance.
It is inevitable in a day when whole classes that never
read before begin to read. The danger lies in the attitude of these new readers, and many old ones, toward
their fiction. For they, too, condescend even when

most hungry for stories. They, too, share the inherited opinion that a novel is only a novel, after all, to be read, but not to be respected, to be squeezed for its juices, then dropped like a grape-skin and forgotten. Perhaps the Elizabethan mob felt much the same way about the plays they crowded to see; but their respect, the critics' respect, Shakespeare's respect, for the language of noble poesy, for noble words and deeds enshrined in poetry, is not paralleled to-day by an appreciation of the fine art of imaginative character representation as it appears in our novel and in all good fiction.

Is it necessary to prove this public disrespect? The terms in which novels are described by their sponsors is proof enough in itself. Seemingly, everything that is reputable must be claimed for every novel—good workmanship, vitality, moral excellence, relative superiority, absolute greatness—in order to secure for it any deference whatsoever. Or, from another angle, how many readers buy novels, and buy them to keep? How many modern novels does one find well bound, and placed on the shelves devoted to "standard reading"? In these Olympian fields a mediocre biography, a volume of second-rate poems, a rehash of history, will find their way before the novels that in the last decade have equaled, if not outranked, the rest of our creative literature.

If more proof were needed, the curious predilections of the serious-minded among our novel-readers would supply it. For not all Americans take the novel too lightly; some take it as heavily as death. To the school that tosses off and away the latest comer is opposed the school which, despising all frivolous stories written for pleasure merely, speaks in tense, devoted breath of those narratives wherein fiction is weighted with facts, and pinned by a moral to the sober side of life. It is significant that the novels most highly respected in America are studies of social conditions, reflexes of politics, or tales where the criticism of morals overshadows the narrative. Here the novel is an admirable agent. Its use as a purveyor of miscellaneous ideas upon things in general is no more objectionable than the cutting of young spruces to serve as Christmastrees. For such a function they were not created, but they make a good end, nevertheless. The important inference is rather that American readers who do pretend to take the novel seriously are moved not so much by the fiction in their narratives as by the sociology, philosophy, or politics imaginatively portrayed. They respect a story with such a content because it comes as near as the novel can to not being fiction at all. And this, I imagine, is an unconscious throw-back to the old days when serious-minded readers chose Hannah More for the place of honor, because her stories taught the moralist how to live and die.

The historically minded will probably remark upon these general conclusions that a certain condescension toward some form of literature has ever been predictable of the general reader; the practically minded may add that no lasting harm to the mind of man and the pursuit of happiness seems to have come of it. The first I freely admit; the second I gravely doubt for the present and distrust for the future. Under conditions as we have them and will increasingly have them here in America, under democratic conditions, condescension toward fiction, the most democratic of literary arts, is certainly dangerous. It is dangerous because it discourages good writing. In this reading society that we have made for ourselves here and in western Europe, where much inspiration, more knowledge, and a fair share of the joy of living come from the printed page, good writing is clearly more valuable than ever before in the history of the race. I do not agree with the pessimists who think that a democratic civilization is necessarily an enemy to fine writing for the public. Such critics underrate the challenge which these millions of minds to be reached and souls to be touched must possess for the courageous author; they forget that writers, like actors, are inspired by a crowded house. But the thought and the labor and the pain that lie behind good writing are doubly difficult in an atmosphere of easy tolerance and good-natured condescension on the part of the readers of the completed work.

The novel is the test case for democratic literature. We cannot afford to pay its practitioners with cash merely, for cash discriminates in quantity and little more. Saul and David were judged by the numbers of their thousands slain; but the test was a crude one for them and cruder still for fiction. We cannot afford to patronize these novelists as our ancestors did before us. Not prizes or endowments or coterie worship or, certainly, more advertising is what the American novelist requires, but a greater respect for his craft. The Elizabethan playwright was frequently despised of the learned world, and, if a favorite with the vulgar, not always a respected one. Strange that learned and vulgar alike should repeat the fallacy in dispraising the preëminently popular art of our own times! To Sir Francis Bacon "Hamlet" was presumably only a play-actor's play. If the great American story should arrive at last, would we not call it "only a novel"?

The Essence of Popularity

You might suppose that popular literature was a modern invention. Cultivated shoulders shrug at the mention of "best sellers" with that air of "the world is going to the devil" which just now is annoyingly familiar. Serious minded people write of *The Saturday Evening Post* as if it represented some new fanaticism destined to wreck civilization. The excessive popularity of so many modern novels is felt to be a mystery.

Of course there are new elements in literary popularity. The wave of interest used to move more slowly. Now thousands, and sometimes millions, read the popular story almost simultaneously, and see it, just a little later on the films. Millions, also, of the class which never used to read at all are accessible to print and have the moving pictures to help them.

But popularity has not changed its fundamental characteristics. The sweep of one man's idea or fancy through other minds, kindling them to interest, has been typical since communication began. The Greek romances of Heliodorus may be analyzed for their popular elements quite as readily as "If Winter Comes." "Pilgrim's Progress" and "The Thousand and One Nights" could serve as models for success, and the question, What makes popularity in fiction? be

56

answered from them with close, if not complete, reference to the present. However, the results of an inquiry into popularity will be surer if we stick to modern literature, not forgetting its historical background. Human nature, which changes its essence so slowly through the centuries, nevertheless shows rapid alterations of phase. The question I propose, therefore, is, What makes a novel popular in our time?

I do not ask it for sordid reasons. What makes a novel sell 100,000 copies, or a short story bring $1000? may seem the same query; but it does not get the same answer, or, apparently, any answer valuable for criticism. A cloud descends upon the eyes of those who try to teach how to make money out of literature and blinds them. Their books go wrong from the start, and most of them are nearly worthless. They propose to teach the sources of popularity, yet instead of dealing with those fundamental qualities of emotion and idea which (as I hope to show) make popularity, their tale is all of emphasis, suspense, beginnings and endings, the relativity of characters, dialogue, setting—useful points for the artisan but not the secret of popularity, nor, it may be added, of greatness in literature. Technique is well enough, in fact some technique is indispensable for a book that is to be popular, but it is the workaday factor in literature, of itself it accomplishes nothing.

But technique can be taught. That is the explanation of the hundred books upon it, and their justification. You cannot teach observation, or sympathy, or the background of knowledge which makes possible the interpretation and selection of experience—not at least in a lesson a week for nine months. Hence literary advisers who must teach something and teach it quickly are drawn, sometimes against their better judgment, to write books on technique by which criticism profits little. Technical perfection becomes their equivalent for excellence and for popularity. It is not an equivalent. More than a mason is required for the making of a statue.

I disclaim any attempt to teach how to be popular in this essay, although deductions may be made. I am interested in popularity as a problem for criticism. I am interested in appraising the pleasure to be got from such popular novels as "The Age of Innocence," "Miss Lulu Bett," "If Winter Comes," or "The Turmoil"— and the not infrequent disappointments from others equally popular. I am especially interested in the attempt to estimate real excellence, an attempt which requires that the momentarily popular shall be separated from the permanently good; which requires that a distinction be made between what must have some excellence because so many people like it, and what is good in a book whether many people like it or not. Such discrimination may not help the young novelist to make money, but it can refine judgment and deepen appreciation.

As for the popularity and its meaning, there need be no quarrel over that term. Let us rule out such accidents as when a weak book becomes widely known because it is supposed to be indecent, or because it is the first to embody popular propaganda, or because its hero is identified with an important figure of real life, or for any other casual reason. If a novel, because of the intrinsic interest of its story, or on account of the contagion of the idea it contains, is widely read by many kinds of readers, and if these readers on their own initiative recommend the book they have read to others, that is popularity, and a sufficient definition.

Perfection of form is not enough to make a book popular. A story has to move or few will read it, but it is doubtful whether a greater technical achievement than this is required for popularity. "Samson Agonistes" is technically perfect, but was never popular, while, to pass from the sublime to its opposite, "This Side of Paradise" was most crudely put together, and yet was popular. The best-built short stories of the past decade have not been the most popular, have not even been the best. No popular writer but could have been (so I profoundly believe) more popular if he had written better. But good writing is not a specific for unpopularity. The excellent writing of Howells could not give him Mark Twain's audience. The weak and tedious construction of Shakespeare's "Antony and Cleopatra," the flat style of Harold Bell Wright's narratives, has not prevented them from being liked. Form is only a first step toward popularity.

Far more important is an appeal to the emotions, which good technique can only make more strong. But what is an appeal to the emotions? "Uncle Tom's

Cabin" appealed to the emotions, and so does "Get-Rich-Quick Wallingford." To what emotions does the popular book appeal? What makes "Treasure Island" popular? Why did "Main Street" have such an unexpected and still reverberating success?

"Treasure Island" is popular because it stirs and satisfies two instinctive cravings of mankind, the love of romantic adventure, and the desire for sudden wealth. This is not true, or rather it is not the whole, or even the important, truth, in "Main Street." There the chief appeal is to an idea not an instinct. We left the war nationally self-conscious as perhaps never before, acutely conscious of the contrasts between our habits, our thinking, our pleasures, our beliefs, and those of Europe. When the soldiers oversea talked generalities at all it was usually of such topics. The millions that never went abroad were plucked from their Main Streets, and herded through great cities to the mingled companionship of the camps. "Main Street," when it came to be written, found an awakened consciousness of provincialism, and a detached view of the home town such as had never before been shared by many. Seeing home from without was so general as to constitute, not a mere experience, but a mass emotion. And upon this new conception, this prejudice against every man's Main Street, the book grasped, and thrived. In like manner, "Uncle Tom's Cabin" grew great upon its conception of slavery. "Robert Elsmere" swept the country because of its exploitation of freedom in religious thought. No one of these books could have been written, or would have been popular if they had been written, before their precise era; no one is likely long to survive it, except as a social document which scholars will read and historians quote.

Roughly then, the appeal which makes for popularity is either to the instinctive emotions permanent in all humanity, though changing shape with circumstances, or to the fixed ideas of the period, which may often and justly be called prejudice. A book may gain its popularity either way, but the results of the first are more likely to be enduring. "Paradise Lost," the least popular of popular poems, still stirs the instinctive craving for heroic revolt, and lives for that quite as much as for the splendors of its verse. Dryden's "Hind and the Panther," which exploited the prejudices of its times, and was popular then, is almost dead.

What are these instinctive cravings that seek satisfaction in fiction and, finding it, make both great and little books popular? Let me list a few without attempting to be complete.

First in importance probably is the desire to escape from reality into a more interesting life. This is a foundation, of course, of all romantic stories, and is part of the definition of the romantic, but it applies to much in literature that is not usually regarded as romance. A more interesting life than yours or mine does not mean one we should wish actually to live, otherwise it would be difficult to account for the taste for detective stories of many sedentary bank presidents; nor does it mean necessarily a beautiful, a wild, a romantic life. No, we wish to escape to any imagined life that will satisfy desires suppressed by circumstance, or incapable of development in any attainable reality.

This desire to escape is eternal, the variety differs with the individual and still more with the period. While youthful love, or romantic adventure as in "Treasure Island," has been an acceptable mode for literature at least as far back as the papyrus tales of the Egyptians, more precise means of delivery from the intolerable weight of real life appear and disappear in popular books. In the early eighteen hundreds, men and women longed to be blighted in love, to be in lonely revolt against the prosaic well-being of a world of little men. Byron was popular. In the Augustan age of England, classic antiquity was a refuge for the dreaming spirit; in Shakespeare's day, Italy; in the fifteenth century, Arthurian romance. Just at present, and in America, the popularity of a series of novels like "The Beautiful and Damned," "The Wasted Generation," "Erik Dorn," and "Cytherea," seems to indicate that many middle-aged readers wish to experience vicariously the alcoholic irresponsibility of a society of "flappers," young graduates, and country club rakes, who threw the pilot overboard as soon as they left the war zone and have been cruising wildly ever since. We remember that for a brief period in the England of Charles II, James II, and William and Mary, rakishness in the plays of Wycherley and Congreve had a glamour of romance upon it and was popular. Indeed, the novel or drama that gives to a generation the escape it desires will always be popular. Test Harold Bell Wright or Zane Grey, Rudyard Kipling or Walter Scott, by this maxim, and it will further define itself, and ring true.

Another human craving is the desire to satisfy the impulses of sex. This is much more difficult to define than the first because it spreads in one phase or another through all cravings. Romance of course has its large sex element, and so have the other attributes to be spoken of later. However, there is a direct and concentrated interest in the relations between the sexes which, in its finer manifestations, seeks for a vivid contrast of personalities in love; in its cruder forms desires raw passion; in its pathological state craves the indecent. A thousand popular novels illustrate the first phase; many more, of which the cave-man story, the desert island romance, "The Sheik" and its companions are examples, represent the second; the ever-surging undercurrent of pornography springs to satisfy the third.

Many sex stories are popular simply because they satisfy curiosity, but curiosity in a broader sense is a human craving which deserves a separate category. Popular novels seldom depend upon it entirely, but they profit by it, sometimes hugely. A novel like Dos Passos's "Three Soldiers," or Mrs. Wharton's "Age of Innocence," or Mrs. Atherton's "Sleeping Fires," makes its first, though not usually its strongest, appeal to our curiosity as to how others live or were living. This was the strength of the innumerable New England, creole, mountaineer, Pennsylvania Dutch stories in the flourishing days of local color. It is a prop of the historical novel and a strong right arm for the picture melodrama of the underworld or the West. Indeed, the pictures, by supplying a photographic background of real scenes inaccessible to the audience have gained a point upon the written story.

Curiosity is a changeable factor, a sure play for immediate popularity, but not to be depended upon for long life. It waxes and wanes and changes its object. Just now we are curious about Russia, the South Sea Islanders, and night life on Broadway; to-morrow it may be New Zealand and Australia, the Argentine millionaire, and quite certainly the Chinese and China. Books appealing to the craving for escape have a longer life, for a story that takes a generation out of itself into fairyland keeps some of its power for the next. Nevertheless, the writer who guesses where curious minds are reaching and gives them what they want, puts money in his purse.

A fourth craving, which is as general as fingers and toes, is for revenge. We laugh now at the plays of revenge before "Hamlet," where the stage ran blood, and even the movie audience no longer enjoys a story the single motive of which is physical revenge. Blood for blood means to us either crime or rowdyism. And yet revenge is just as popular in literature now as in the sixteenth century. Only its aspect has changed. Our fathers are not butchered in feuds, our sons are not sold into slavery, and except in war or in street robberies we are not insulted by brute physical force. Nevertheless we are cheated by scoundrels, oppressed by financial tyranny, wounded by injustice, suppressed by self-sufficiency, rasped by harsh tempers, annoyed by snobbery, and often ruined by unconscious selfishness. We long to strike back at the human traits which have wronged us, and the satiric depiction of hateful characters whose seeming virtues are turned upside down to expose their impossible hearts feeds our craving for vicarious revenge. We dote upon vinegarish old maids, self-righteous men, and canting women when they are exposed by narrative art, and especially when poetic justice wrecks them. The books that contain them bid for popularity. It happens that in rapid succession we have seen three novels in which this element of popular success was strong: Miss Sinclair's "Mr. Waddington of Wyck," "Vera," by the author of "Elizabeth in Her German Garden," and Mr. Hutchinson's "If Winter Comes." The first two books focus upon this quality, and their admirable unity gives them superior force; but it is noteworthy that "If Winter Comes," which adds other popular elements in large measure to its release of hate, has been financially the most successful of the three.

To these deep cravings of the heart must be added another of major importance. I mean aspiration, the deep desire of all human without exception sometimes to be better, nobler, finer, truer. Stories of daring in the face of unconquerable odds, stories of devotion, above all stories of self-sacrifice are made to gratify this emotion. They are purges for the restless soul. Some critic of our short story discovered not long ago that the bulk of the narratives chosen for reprinting had self-sacrifice as theme. This is precisely what one would expect of comfortable, ease-loving peoples, like the Germans before the empire and the Americans of our generation. When no real sacrifice of goods, of energy, of love, or of life is necessary, then the craving for stories of men who give up all and women who efface themselves is particularly active. The hard, individualistic stories of selfish characters—Ben Hecht's for example, and Scott Fitzgerald's—have been written after a war period of enforced self-sacrifice and by young men who were familiar with suffering for a cause. But most American readers of our generation live easily and have always lived easily, and that undoubtedly accounts for the extraordinary popularity here of aspiring books. Reading of a fictitious hero who suffers for others is a tonic for our conscience, and like massage takes the place of exercise. By a twist in the same argument, it may be seen that the cheerful optimist in fiction, who Pollyannawise believes all is for the best, satisfies the craving to justify our well-being. I do not, however, mean to disparage this element of popularity. It is after all the essential quality of tragedy where the soul rises above misfortune. It is a factor in noble literature as well as in popular success.

So much for some of the typical and instinctive cravings which cry for satisfaction and are the causes of popularity. To them may be added others of course, notably the desire for sudden wealth, which is a factor in "Treasure Island" as in all treasure stories, and the prime cause of success in the most popular of all plots, the tale of Cinderella, which, after passing through feudal societies with a prince's hand as reward, changed its sloven sister for a shopgirl and King Cophetua into a millionaire, and swept the American stage. To this may also be added simpler stimulants of instinctive emotion, humor stirring to pleasant laughter, pathos that exercises sympathy, the happy ending that makes for joy. Stories which succeed because they stir and satisfy in this fashion are like opera in a foreign tongue, which moves us even when we do not fully understand the reason for our emotion. They differ from another kind of popular story, in which a popular idea rather than an instinctive emotion is crystallized, and which now must be considered.

Each generation has its fixed ideas. A few are inherited intact by the generation that follows, a few are passed on with slight transformation, but most crumble or change into different versions of the old half-truths. Among the most enduring of prejudices is the fallacy of the good old times. Upon that formula nine-tenths of the successful historical romances are built. That American wives suffer from foreign husbands, that capital is ruthless, that youth is right and age wrong, that energy wins over intellect, that virtue is always rewarded, are American conceptions of some endurance that have given short but lofty flights to thousands of native stories.

More important, however, in the history of fiction are those wide and slow moving currents of opinion, for which prejudice is perhaps too narrow a name, which flow so imperceptibly through the minds of a generation or a whole century that there is little realization of their novelty. Such a slow-moving current was the humanitarianism which found such vigorous expression in Dickens, the belief in industrial democracy which is being picked up as a theme by novelist after novelist to-day, or the sense of the value of personality and human experience which so intensely characterizes the literature of the early Renaissance.

If a novel draws up into itself one of these ideas, filling it with emotion, it gains perhaps its greatest assurance of immediate popularity. If the idea is of vast social importance, this popularity may continue. But if it is born of immediate circumstance, like the hatred of slavery in "Uncle Tom's Cabin," or if it is still more transient, say, the novelty of a new invention, like the airplane or wireless, then the book grows stale with its theme. The like is true of a story that teaches a lesson a generation are willing to be taught—it lives as long as the lesson. What has become of Charles Kingsley's novels, of the apologues of Maria Edgeworth? "Main Street" is such a story; so was "Mr. Britling Sees It Through"; so probably "A Doll's House." Decay is already at their hearts. Only the student knows how many like tales that preached fierily a text for the times have died in the past. But I am writing of popularity not of permanence. In four popular novels out of five, even in those where the appeal to the instinctive emotions is dominant, suspect some prejudice of the times embodied and usually exploited. It is the most potent of lures for that ever increasing public which has partly trained intelligence as well as emotions.

Perhaps it is already clear that most popular novels combine many elements of popularity, although usually one is dominant. Among the stories, for instance, which I have mentioned most frequently, "Main Street" depends upon a popular idea, but makes use also of the revenge motive. It is not at all, as many hasty critics said, an appeal to curiosity. We know our Main Streets well enough already. And therefore in England, which also was not curious about Main Streets, and where the popular idea that Sinclair Lewis seized upon was not prevalent, the book has had only a moderate success. "If Winter Comes" combines the revenge motive with aspiration. Scott Fitzgerald's first novel made its strong appeal to curiosity. We had heard of the wild younger generation and were curious. His second book depends largely upon the craving for sex experience, in which it resembles Mr. Hergesheimer's "Cytherea," but also plays heavily upon the motive of escape, and upon sheer curiosity. "Miss Lulu Bett" was a story of revenge. Booth Tarkington's "Alice Adams"—to bring in a new title—is a good illustration of a story where for once a popular novelist slurred over the popular elements in order to concentrate upon a study of character. His book received tardy recognition but it disappointed his less critical admirers. Mr. White's "Andivius Hedulio" depends for its popularity upon curiosity and escape.

The popular story, then, the financially successful, the immediately notorious story, should appeal to the instinctive emotions and may be built upon popular prejudice. What is the moral for the writer? Is he to lay out the possible fields of emotion as a surveyor prepares for his blue print? By no means. Unless he follows his own instinct in the plan, or narrates because of his own excited thinking he will produce a thinly clad formula rather than a successful story. There is no moral for the writer, only some rays of light thrown upon the nature of his achievement. The way to accomplish popularity, if that is what you want, is to write for the people, and let formula, once it is understood, take care of itself. As an editor, wise in popularity, once said to me, "Oppenheim and the rest are popular because they think like the people not for them."

What is the moral of this discussion for the critical reader? A great one, for if he does not wish to be tricked constantly by his own emotions into supposing that what is timely is therefore fine, and what moves him is therefore great, he must distinguish between the elements of popularity and the essence of greatness. It is evident, I think, from the argument that every element of popularity described above may be made effective upon our weak human nature with only an approximation to truth. The craving for escape may be, and usually is, answered by sentimental romance, where every emotion, from patriotism to amorousness, is mawkish and unreal. Every craving may be played upon in the same fashion just because it is a craving, and the result be often more popular for the exaggeration. Also it is notorious that a prejudice—or a popular idea, if you prefer the term—which is seized upon for fiction, almost inevitably is strained beyond logic and beyond truth, so much so that in rapid years, like those of 1916 to 1920 which swept us into propaganda and out again, the emphatic falsity of a book's central thesis may be recognized before the first editions are exhausted. It would be interesting to run off, in the midst of a 1922 performance, some of the war films that stirred audiences of 1918. It will be interesting to reread some of the cheaper and more popular war stories that carried even you, O judicious reader, off your even balance not five years ago to-day!

We have always known, of course, that a novel can be highly popular without being truly excellent. Nevertheless, it is a valuable discipline to specify the reasons. And it is good discipline also in estimating the intrinsic value of a novel to eliminate as far as is possible the temporal and the accidental; and in particular the especial appeal it may have to your own private craving—for each of us has his soft spot where the pen can pierce. On the contrary, if the highly speculative business of guessing the probable circulation of a novel ever becomes yours, then you must

doubly emphasize the importance of these very qualities; search for them, analyze them out of the narrative, equate them with the tendencies of the times, the
new emotions stirring, the new interests, new thoughts
abroad, and then pick best sellers in advance.

Yet in eliminating the accidental in the search for
real excellence, it would be disastrous to eliminate all
causes of popularity with it. That would be to assume
that the good story cannot be popular, which is nonsense. The best books are nearly always popular,
if not in a year, certainly in a decade or a century.
Often they spread more slowly than less solid achievements for the same reason that dear things sell less
rapidly than cheap. The best books cost more to
read because they contain more, and to get much out
the reader must always put much in. Nevertheless, the
good novel will always contain one or more of the
elements of popularity in great intensity. I make but
one exception, and that for those creations of the sheer
intellect, like the delicate analyses of Henry James,
where the appeal is to the subtle mind, and the emotion
aroused an intellectual emotion. Such novels are on
the heights, but they are never at the summit of literary
art. They are limited by the partiality of their appeal,
just as they are exalted by the perfection of their ac-
complishment. They cannot be popular, and are not.

The "best seller" therefore may be great but does
not need to be. It is usually a weak book, no matter
how readable, because ordinarily it has only the elements of popularity to go on, and succeeds by their

number and timeliness instead of by fineness and truth.
A second-rate man can compound a best seller if his
sense for the popular is first-rate. In his books the
instinctive emotions are excited over a broad area, and
arise rapidly to sink again. No better examples can
be found than in the sword-and-buckler romance of
our 'nineties which set us all for a while thinking
feudal thoughts and talking shallow gallantry. Now
it is dead, stone dead. Not even the movies can re-
vive it. The emotions it aroused went flat over night.
Much the same is true of books that trade in prejudice,
like the white slave stories of a decade ago. For a
moment we were stirred to the depths. We swallowed
the concept whole and raged with a furious indigestion
of horrible fact. And then it proved to be colic only.

With such a light ballast of prejudice or sentiment
can the profitable ship popularity be kept upright for
a little voyage, and this, prevailingly, is all her cargo.
But the wise writer, if he is able, as Scott, and Dickens,
and Clemens were able, freights her more deeply. As
for the good reader, he will go below to investigate
before the voyage commences; or, if in midcourse he
likes not his carrier, take off in his mental airplane
and seek another book.

II
On the American Tradition

The American Tradition

I REMEMBER a talk in Dublin with an Irish writer whose English prose has adorned our period. It was 1918, and the eve of forced conscription, and his indignation with English policy was intense. "I will give up their language," he said, "all except Shakespeare. I will write only Gaelic." Unfortunately, he could read Gaelic much better than he could write it. In his heart, indeed, he knew how mad he would have been to give up the only literary tradition which, thanks to language, could be his own; and in a calmer mood since he has enriched that tradition with admirable translations from the Irish. He was suffering from a mild case of Anglomania.

Who is the real Anglomaniac in America? Not the now sufficiently discredited individual with a monocle and a pseudo-Oxford accent, who tries to be more English than the English. Not the more subtly dangerous American who refers his tastes, his enthusiasms, his culture, and the prestige of his compatriots to an English test before he dare assert them. The real Anglomaniac is the American who tries to be less English than his own American tradition. He is the man who is obsessed with the fear of "Anglo-Saxon domination."

How many Anglomaniacs by this definition are at

large in America each reader may judge for himself. Personally, I find them extraordinarily numerous, and of so many varieties, from the mere borrower of opinions to the deeply convinced zealot, that it seems wiser to analyze Anglomania than to discuss the various types that possess it. And in this analysis let us exclude from the beginning such very real, but temporary, grievances against the English as spring from Irish oppressions, trade rivalries, or the provocations which always arise between allies in war. All such causes of anti-English and anti-"Anglo-Saxon" sentiment belong in a different category from the underlying motives which I propose to discuss.

These new Anglomaniacs, with their talk of Anglo-Saxon domination, cannot mean English domination. That would be absurd, although even absurdities are current coin in restless years like these. At least one Irishman of my acquaintance *knows* that King George cabled Wilson to bring America into the war, and that until that cable came Wilson dared not act. I can conceive of an English influence upon literature that is worth attacking, and also worth defending. I can conceive of a far less important English influence upon our social customs. But in neither case, domination. That England dominates our finance, our industry, our politics, is just now, especially, the suspicion of a paranoiac, or the idea of an ignoramus.

"Anglo-Saxon domination," even in an anti-British meeting, cannot and does not mean English domination; it can mean only control of America by the so-called Anglo-Saxon element in our population. The quarrel is local, not international. The "Anglo-Saxon" three thousand miles away who cannot hit back is a scapegoat, a whipping boy for the so-called "Anglo-Saxon" American at home.

What is an "Anglo-Saxon" American? Presumably he is the person familiar in "want" advertisements: "American family wants boarder for the summer. References exchanged." But this does not help us much. He is certainly not English. Nothing is better established than the admixture of bloods since the earliest days of our nationality. That I, myself, for example, have ancestral portions of French, German, Welsh, and Scotch, as well as English blood in my veins, makes me, by any historical test, characteristically more rather than less American. Race, indeed, within very broad limits, is utterly different from nationality, and it is usually many, many centuries before the two become even approximately identical. The culture I have inherited, the political ideals I live by, the literature which is my own, most of all the language that I speak, are far more important than the ultimate race or races I stem from, obviously more important, since in thousands of good Americans it is impossible to determine what races have gone to their making. There is no such thing as an Anglo-Saxon American—and so few English Americans that they are nationally insignificant.

An American with a strong national individuality there certainly is, and it is true that his traditions, irrespective of the race of his forbears, are mainly English; from England he drew his political and social habits, his moral ideas, his literature, and his language. This does not make him a "slave to England," as our most recent propagandists would have it; it does not put him in England's debt. We owe no debt to England. Great Britain, Canada, Australia, New Zealand, South Africa, and ourselves are deeply in debt to our intellectual, our spiritual, our esthetic ancestors who were the molders of English history and English thought, the interpreters of English emotion, the masters of the developing English *mores* that became our *mores,* and have since continued evolution with a difference. Chaucer, Shakespeare, Spenser, and Milton, Wycliffe, Bunyan, Fox, and Wesley, Elizabeth, Cromwell, and the great Whigs, these made the only tradition that can be called Anglo-Saxon, and if we have an American tradition, as we assuredly have, here are its roots. This is our "Anglo-Saxon domination."

But if the roots of this tradition are English, its trunk is thoroughly American, seasoned and developed through two centuries of specifically American history. As we know it to-day it is no longer "Anglo-Saxon," it is as American as our cities, our soil, our accent upon English. If we are going to discuss "domination" let us be accurate and speak of the domination of American tradition. It is against the American tradition that the new Anglomaniac actually protests.

Dominating this American tradition is, dominating, almost tyrannical, for one reason only, but that a strong one, a fact not a convention, a factor, not a mere influence—dominating because of the English language.

In our century language has become once again as powerful as in the Roman Empire—and its effects, thanks to printing and easy transportation, are far more quickly attained. Hordes from all over Europe have swarmed into the domain of English. They have come to a country where the new language was indispensable. They have learned it, or their children have learned it. English has become their means of communication with their neighbors, with business, with the state. Sooner or later even the news of Europe has come to them through English, and sometimes unwillingly, but more often unconsciously, they have come under the American, the real "Anglo-Saxon" domination.

For a language, of course, is more than words. It is a body of literature, it is a method of thinking, it is a definition of emotions, it is the exponent and the symbol of a civilization. You cannot adopt English without adapting yourself in some measure to the English, or the Anglo-American tradition. You cannot adopt English political words, English literary words, English religious words, the terms of sport or ethics, without in some measure remaking your mind on a new model. If you fail or refuse, your child will not. He is forcibly made an American, in ideas at least, and chiefly by language.

I submit that it is impossible for an alien *thoroughly*

to absorb and understand Lincoln's Gettysburg Speech or Hawthorne's "Scarlet Letter" without working a slight but perceptible transformation in the brain, without making himself an heir of a measure of English tradition. And the impact of English as a spoken tongue, and the influence of its literature as the only read literature, are great beyond ordinary conception. Communities where a foreign language is read or spoken only delay the process, they cannot stop it.

The foreigner, it is true, has modified the English language precisely as he has modified the American tradition. Continental Europe is audible in the American tongue, as it is evident in the American mind; but it is like the English or the Spanish touch upon the Gothic style in architecture—there is modification, but not fundamental change.

Many a foreign-born American has been restless under this domination. The letters and memoirs of the French immigrants from revolutionary France express discomfort freely. The Germans of '48, themselves the bearers of a high civilization, have often confessed an unwilling assimilation. The Germans of earlier migrations herded apart like the later Scandinavians, in part to avoid the tyranny of tongue.

Imagine a German coming here in early manhood. His tradition is not English; he owes nothing to a contemporary England that he but dimly knows. Speaking English, perhaps only English, he grows impatient with a tongue every concept of which has an English coloring. The dominance of the language, and especially of its literature, irks him. He no longer wants to think as a German; he wants to think as an American; but the medium of his thought must be English. His anger often enough goes out against English history, English literature. He is easily irritated by England. But it is the American past that binds and is converting him. Such consciousness of the power of environment is perhaps rare, but the fact is common. In our few centuries of history millions have been broken into English, with all that implies. Millions have experienced the inevitable discomfort of a foreign tradition which makes alien their fatherlands, and strangers of their children. This is an "Anglo-Saxon" domination. But it is useless to struggle against it.

There is a similar discomfort among certain American authors, especially just now, when, for the first time since the Civil War and the materialism that succeeded it, we are finding our national self once again in literature. Mr. Mencken and Mr. Dreiser have vigorously expressed this annoyance with American tradition. They wish to break with it—at least Mr. Dreiser does—break with it morally, spiritually, esthetically. Let the dotards, he says, bury their dead.

Mr. Mencken wishes to drive us out of Colonialism. He says that Longfellow has had his day, and that it is time to stop imitating Addison, time to be ashamed of aping Stevenson, Kipling, or John Masefield. He is right.

But when it comes to disowning English literature

and the past of American literature (as many a writer directly or by implication would have us) in order to become 100 per cent American, let us first take breath long enough to reflect that, first, such a madcap career is eminently undesirable, and, second, utterly impossible. It is a literature which by general admission is now the richest and most liberal in the world of living speech. English is a tongue less sonorous than Italian, less fine than French, less homely than German, but more expressive, more flexible, than these and all others. Its syntax imposes no burdens, its traditions are weighty only upon the vulgar and the bizarre. Without its literary history, American literature in general, and usually in particular, is not to be understood. That we have sprung from a Puritanical loin, and been nourished in the past from the breast of Victorianism, is obvious. In this we have been not too much, but too narrowly, English. We have read Tennyson when it might have been better to have read Shakespeare or Chaucer. But to wish to break with English literature in order to become altogether American is like desiring to invent an entirely new kind of clothes. I shall not give up trousers because my fourth great-grandfather, who was a Yorkshireman, wore them, and his pattern no longer fits my different contour. I shall make me a pair better suiting my own shanks—yet they shall still be trousers. But in any case, language binds us.

Indeed, in this welter of newcomers here in America, whose children learn, read, write only English, the tradition of Anglo-American literature is all that holds us by a thread above chaos. If we could all be made to speak German, or Italian, or Spanish, there would be cause, but no excuse, for an attempted revolution. But English is dominant here and will remain so. Could we hope to make an American literary language without dependence on English literature, a protective tariff on home-made writing, or an embargo against books more than a year old, or imported from across the Atlantic, would be worth trying; but the attempts so far are not encouraging. This has not been the way in the past by which original literatures have been made. They have sucked nourishment where it could best be found, and grown great from the strength that good food gave them.

One can sympathize with the desire to nationalize our literature at all costs; and can understand lashings out at the tyranny of literary prestige which England still exercises. But the real question is: shall the English of Americans be good English or bad English; shall a good tradition safeguard change and experiment, or shall we have chaotic vulgarity like the Low Latin of the late Roman Empire?

The truth is that our language *is* tradition, for it holds tradition in solution like iron in wine. And here lie the secret and the power of American, "Anglo-Saxon" domination.

What is to be done about it? Shall anything be done about it? The Anglomaniac is helpless before the fact of language. The most he can do is to attack, and uproot if he can, the American tradition.

There is nothing sacrosanct in this American tradition. Like all traditions it is stiff, it will clasp, if we allow it, the future in the dead hand of precedent. It can be used by the designing to block progress. But as traditions go it is not conservative. Radicalism, indeed, is its child. Political and religious radicalism brought the Pilgrims to New England, the Quakers to Pennsylvania; political and economic radicalism made the Revolution against the will of American conservatives; political and social radicalism made the Civil War inevitable and gave it moral earnestness. Radicalism, whether you like it or not, is much more American than what some people mean by "Americanism" to-day. And its bitterest opponents in our times would quite certainly have become Nova Scotian exiles if they had been alive and likeminded in 1783.

Nor is this American tradition impeccable in the political ideas, the literary ideals, the social customs it has given us. We must admit a rampant individualism in our political practices which is in the very best Anglo-American tradition, and yet by no means favorable to coöperative government. We admit also more Puritanism in our standard literature than art can well digest; and more sentiment than is good for us; nor is it probable that the traditions and the conventions which govern American family life are superior to their European equivalents. We should welcome (I do not say that we do) liberalizing, broad-

ening, enriching influences from other traditions. And
whether we have welcomed them or not, they have
come, and to our great benefit. But to graft upon
the plant is different from trying to pull up the roots.

We want better arguments than the fear of Anglo-
Saxon domination before the root pulling begins. We
wish to know what is to be planted. We desire to
be convinced that the virtue has gone out of the old
stock. We want examples of civilized nations that
have profited by borrowing traditions wholesale, or by
inventing them. We wish to know if a cultural, a
literary sans-culottism is possible, except with chaos
as a goal. Most of all, we expect to fight for and to
hold our Anglo-American heritage.

It is not surprising that discontent with our own
ultimately English tradition has expressed itself by a
kind of Freudian transformation in anti-English sentiment. Every vigorous nation strains and struggles with
its tradition, like a growing boy with his clothes, and
this is particularly true of new nations with old traditions behind them. Our pains are growing pains—a
malady we have suffered from since the early eighteenth
century at the latest. Tradition, our own tradition,
pinches us; but you cannot punch tradition for pinching you, or call it names to its face, especially if it proves
to be your father's tradition, or your next-door neighbor's. Therefore, since that now dim day when the
Colonies acquired a self-consciousness of their own,
many good Americans have chosen England and the
English to symbolize whatever irked them in their

own tradition. It is from England and the English that we have felt ourselves growing away, from which we had to grow away in order to be ourselves and not a shadow—imitators, second-bests, Colonials. England and the English have had our vituperation whenever the need to be American has been greatest. And when an English government like Palmerston's, or Salisbury's, or Lloyd George's, offends some group or race among us, a lurking need to assert our individuality, or prove that we are not Colonials, leads thousands more to join in giving the lion's tail an extra twist.

This may be unfortunate, but it argues curiously enough respect and affection rather than the reverse, and it is very human. It is a fact, like growing, and is likely to continue until we are fully grown. It will reassert itself vehemently until upon our English tradition we shall have built an American civilization as definitely crystallized, a literature as rich and self-sufficing, as that of France and England to-day. Three-quarters of our national genius went into the creating of our political system. Three-quarters of our national genius since has gone into the erecting of our economic system. Here we are independent—and thick skinned. But a national civilization and a national literature take more time to complete.

Cool minds were prepared for a little tail-twisting after the great war, even though they could not foresee the unfortunate Irish situation in which a British government seemed determined to make itself as un-English as possible. If there had not been the patriotic urge to assert our essential Americanism more strongly than ever, there still would have been a reaction against all the pledging and the handshaking, the pother about blood and water, the purple patches in every newspaper asserting Anglo-Saxonism against the world. I remember my own nervousness when, in 1918, after the best part of a year in England, in England's darkest days, I came back full of admiration for the pluck of all England and the enlightenment of her best minds in the great struggle, to hear men who knew little of England orating of enduring friendship, and to read writers who had merely read of England, descanting of her virtues. I felt, and many felt, that excess of ignorant laudation which spells certain reaction into ignorant dispraise. No wonder that Americans whose parents happened to be Germans, Italians, Jews, or Irish grew weary of hearing of the essential virtues of the Anglo-Saxon race. There never was such a race. It was not even English blood, but English institutions that created America; but Liberty Loan orators had no time to make fine distinctions of that kind. They talked, and even while the cheers were ringing and the money rolled in dissent raised its tiny head.

Dissent was to be expected; antagonism against a tradition made by English minds and perpetuated in English was natural after a war in which not merely nationalism, but also every racial instinct, has been quickened and made sensitive. But *tout comprendre, c'est tout pardonner*, is only partly true in this instance. We should understand, and be tolerant with, the strainings against tradition of folk to whom it is still partly alien; we should diagnose our own growing pains and not take them too seriously. Nevertheless, the better more violent movements of race and national prejudice are understood, the less readily can they be pardoned, if by pardon one means easy tolerance.

It is not inconceivable that we shall have to face squarely a split between those who prefer the American tradition and those who do not, although where the cleavage line would run, whether between races or classes, is past guessing. There are among us apparently men and women who would risk wars, external or internal, in order to hasten the discordant day; although just what they expect as a result, whether an Irish-German state organized by German efficiency and officered by graduates of Tammany Hall, or a pseudo-Russian communism, is not yet clear. In any case, the time is near when whoever calls himself American will have to take his stand and do more thinking, perhaps, than was necessary in 1917. He will need to know what tradition is, what his own consists of, and what he would do without it. He will need especially to rid himself of such simple and fallacious ideas as that what was good enough for his grandfather is good enough for him; or that, as some of our more reputable newspapers profess to think, the Constitution has taken the place once held by the Bible, and contains the whole duty of man and all that is necessary for his welfare. He will need to think less of 100 per cent Americanism, which, as it is commonly used, means not to think at all, and more of how he himself is molding American tradition for the generation that is to follow. If he is not to be a pawn merely in the struggle for American unity, he must think more clearly and deeply than has been his habit in the past.

But whatever happens in America (and after the sad experiences of prophets in the period of war and reconstruction, who would prophesy), let us cease abusing England whenever we have indigestion in our own body politic. It is seemingly inevitable that the writers of vindictive editorials should know little more of England as she is to-day than of Russia or the Chinese Republic; inevitable, apparently, that for them the Irish policy of the Tory group in Parliament, Indian unrest, and Lloyd George, are all that one needs to known about a country whose liberal experiments in industrial democracy since the war, and whose courage in reconstruction, may well make us hesitate in dispraise. But it is not inevitable that Americans who are neither headline and editorial writers, nor impassioned orators, regardless of facts, should continue to damn the English because their ancestors and ours founded America.

Back to Nature

No one tendency in life as we live it in America to-day is more characteristic than the impulse, as recurrent as summer, to take to the woods. Sometimes it disguises itself under the name of science; sometimes it is mingled with hunting and the desire to kill; often it is sentimentalized and leads strings of gaping "students" bird-hunting through the wood lot; and again it perilously resembles a desire to get back from civilization and go "on the loose." Say your worst of it, still the fact remains that more Americans go back to nature for one reason or another annually than any civilized men before them. And more Americans, I fancy, are studying nature in clubs or public schools —or, in summer camps and the Boy Scouts, imitating nature's creatures, the Indian and the pioneer—than even statistics could make believable.

What is the cause? In life, it is perhaps some survival of the pioneering instinct, spending itself upon fishing, or bird-hunting, or trail hiking, much as the fight instinct leads us to football, or the hunt instinct sends every dog sniffing at dawn through the streets of his town. Not every one is thus atavistic, if this be atavism; not every American is sensitive to spruce spires, or the hermit thrush's chant, or white water in a forest gorge, or the meadow lark across the frosted fields. Naturally. The surprising fact is that in a bourgeois civilization like ours, so many are affected.

And yet what a criterion nature love or nature indifference is. It seems that if I can try a man by a silent minute in the pines, the view of a jay pirating through the bushes, spring odors, or December flush on evening snow, I can classify him by his reactions. Just where I do not know; for certainly I do not put him beyond the pale if his response is not as mine. And yet he will differ, I feel sure, in more significant matters. He is not altogether of my world. Nor does he enter into this essay. There are enough without him, and of every class. In the West, the very day laborer pitches his camp in the mountains for his two weeks' holiday. In the East and Middle West, every pond with a fringe of hemlocks, or hill view by a trolley line, or strip of ocean beach, has its cluster of bungalows where the proletariat perform their *villeggiatura* as the Italian aristocracy did in the days of the Renaissance. Patently the impulse exists, and counts for something here in America.

It counts for something, too, in American literature. Since our writing ceased being colonial English and began to reflect a race in the making, the note of woods-longing has been so insistent that one wonders whether here is not to be found at last the characteristic "trait" that we have all been patriotically seeking.

I do not limit myself in this statement to the professed "nature writers" of whom we have bred far more than any other race with which I am familiar. In the list—which I shall not attempt—of the greatest American writers, one cannot fail to include Emerson, Hawthorne, Thoreau, Cooper, Lowell, and Whitman. And every one of these men was vitally concerned with nature, and some were obsessed by it. Lowell was a scholar and man of the world, urban therefore; but his poetry is more enriched by its homely New England background than by its European polish. Cooper's ladies and gentlemen are puppets merely, his plots melodrama; it is the woods he knew, and the creatures of the woods, Deerslayer and Chingachgook, that preserve his books. Whitman made little distinction between nature and human nature, perhaps too little. But read "Out of the Cradle Endlessly Rocking" or "The Song of the Redwood-Tree," and see how keen and how vital was his instinct for native soil. As for Hawthorne, you could make a text-book on nature study from his "Note-Books." He was an imaginative moralist first of all; but he worked out his visions in terms of New England woods and hills. So did Emerson. The day was "not wholly profane" for him when he had "given heed to some natural object." Thoreau needs no proving. He is at the forefront of all field and forest lovers in all languages and times.

These are the greater names. The lesser are as leaves in the forest: Audubon, Burroughs, Muir, Clarence King, Lanier, Robert Frost, and many more— the stream broadening and shallowing through literary scientists and earnest forest lovers to romantic "nature fakers," literary sportsmen, amiable students, and tens of thousands of teachers inculcating this American tendency in another generation. The phenomenon asks for an explanation. It is more than a category of American literature that I am presenting; it *is* an American trait.

The explanation I wish to proffer in this essay may sound fantastical; most explanations that explain anything usually do—at first. I believe that this vast rush of nature into American literature is more than a mere reflection of a liking for the woods. It represents a search for a tradition, and its capture.

Good books, like well-built houses, must have tradition behind them. The Homers and Shakespeares and Goethes spring from rich soil left by dead centuries; they are like native trees that grow so well nowhere else. The little writers—hacks who sentimentalize to the latest order, and display their plot novelties like bargains on an advertising page—are just as traditional. The only difference is that their tradition goes back to books instead of life. Middle-sized authors—the very good and the probably enduring—are successful largely because they have gripped a tradition and followed it through to contemporary life. This is what Thackeray did in "Vanity Fair," Howells in "The Rise of Silas Lapham," and Mrs. Wharton in "The House of Mirth." But the back-to-nature books—both the sound ones and those shameless exposures of the private emotions of ground hogs and turtles that call themselves nature books—are the most traditional of all. For they plunge directly into what might be called the adventures of the American sub-consciousness.

It is the sub-consciousness that carries tradition into literature. That curious reservoir where forgotten experiences lie waiting in every man's mind, as vivid as on the day of first impression, is the chief concern of psychologists nowadays. But it has never yet had due recognition from literary criticism. If the sub-consciousness is well stocked, a man writes truly, his imagination is vibrant with human experience, he sets his own humble observation against a background of all he has learned and known and forgotten of civilization. If it is under-populated, if he has done little, felt little, known little of the traditional experiences of the intellect, he writes thinly. He can report what he sees, but it is hard for him to create. It was Chaucer's rich sub-consciousness that turned his simple little story of Chauntecleer into a comment upon humanity. Other men had told that story—and made it scarcely more than trivial. It is the promptings of forgotten memories in the sub-consciousness that give to a simple statement the force of old, unhappy things, that keep thoughts true to experience, and test fancy by life. The sub-consciousness is the governor of the waking brain. Tradition—which is just man's memory of man—flows through it like an underground river from which rise the springs of every-day thinking. If there is anything remarkable about a book, look to the sub-consciousness of the writer and study the racial tradition that it bears.

Now, I am far from proposing to analyze the American sub-consciousness. No man can define it. But of this much I am certain. The American habit of going "back to nature" means that in our sub-consciousness nature is peculiarly active. We react to nature as does no other race. We are the descendants of pioneers—all of us. And if we have not inherited a memory of pioneering experiences, at least we possess inherited tendencies and desires. The impulse that drove Boone westward may nowadays do no more than send some young Boone canoeing on Temagami, or push him up Marcy or Shasta to inexplicable happiness on the top. But the drive is there. And furthermore, nature is still strange in America. Even now the wilderness is far from no American city. Birds, plants, trees, even animals have not, as in Europe, been absorbed into the common knowledge of the race. There are discoveries everywhere for those who can make them. Nature, indeed, is vivid in a surprising number of American brain cells, marking them with a deep and endurable impress. And our flood of nature books has served to increase her power.

It was never so with the European traditions that we brought to America with us. That is why no one reads early American books. They are pallid, ill-nourished, because their traditions are pallid. They drew upon the least active portion of the American sub-consciousness, and reflect memories not of experience, contact, live thought, but of books. Even Washington Irving, our first great author, is not free from this indictment. If, responding to some obscure drift of his race towards humor and the short story, he had not ripened his Augustan inheritance upon an American hillside, he, too, would by now seem juiceless, withered, like a thousand cuttings from English stock planted in forgotten pages of his period. It was not until the end of our colonial age and the rise of democracy towards Jackson's day, that the rupture with our English background became sufficiently complete to make us fortify pale memories of home by a search for fresher, more vigorous tradition.

We have been searching ever since, and many eminent critics think that we have still failed to establish American literature upon American soil. The old traditions, of course, were essential. Not even the most self-sufficient American hopes to establish a brand-new culture. The problem has been to domesticate Europe, not to get rid of her. But the old stock needed a graft, just as an old fruit tree needs a graft. It requires a new tradition. We found a tradition in New England; and then New England was given over to the alien and her traditions became local or historical merely. We found another in border life; and then the Wild West reached the Pacific and vanished. Time and again we have been flung back upon our English sources, and forced to imitate a literature sprung from a riper soil. Of course, this criticism, as it stands, is too sweeping. It neglects Mark Twain and the tradition of the American boy; it neglects Walt Whitman and the literature of free and turbulent democracy; it neglects Longfellow and Poe and that romantic tradition of love and beauty common to all Western races. But, at least, it makes one understand why the American writer has passionately sought anything that would put an American quality into his transplanted style.

He has been very successful in local color. But then local color is *local*. It is a minor art. In the field of human nature he has fought a doubtful battle. An occasional novel has broken through into regions where it is possible to be utterly American even while writing English. Poems too have followed. But here lie our great failures. I do not speak of the "great American novel," yet to come. I refer to the absence of a school of American fiction, or poetry, or drama, that has linked itself to any tradition broader than the romance of the colonies, New England of the 'forties, or the East Side of New York. The men who most often write for all America are mediocre. They strike no deeper than a week-old interest in current activity. They aim to hit the minute because they are shrewd enough to see that for "all America" there is very little continuity just now between one minute and the next. The America they write for is contemptuous of tradition, although worshipping convention, which is the tradition of the ignorant. The men who write for a fit audience though few are too often local or archaic, narrow or European, by necessity if not by choice.

And ever since we began to incur the condescension of foreigners by trying to be American, we have been conscious of this weak-rootedness in our literature and trying to remedy it. This is why our flood of nature books for a century is so significant. They may seem peculiar instruments for probing tradition—particularly the sentimental ones. The critic has not yet admitted some of the heartiest among them—Audubon's sketches of pioneer life, for example—into literature at all. And yet, unless I am mightily mistaken, they are signs of convalescence as clearly as they are symptoms of our disease. These United States, of course, are infinitely more important than the plot of mother earth upon which they have been erected. The intellectual background that we have inherited from Europe is more significant than the moving spirit of woods and soil and waters here. The graft, in truth, is less valuable than the tree upon which it is grafted. Yet it determines the fruit. So with the books of our nature lovers. They represent a passionate attempt to acclimatize the breed. Thoreau has been one of our most original writers. He and his multitudinous followers, wise and foolish, have helped establish us in our new soil.

I may seem to exaggerate the services of a group of writers who, after all, can show but one great name, Thoreau's. I do not think so, for if the heart of the nature lover is sometimes more active than his head,

the earth intimacies he gives us are vital to literature
in a very practical sense. Thanks to the modern science of geography, we are beginning to understand
the profound and powerful influence of physical environment upon men. The geographer can tell you
why Charleston was aristocratic, why New York is
hurried and nervous, why Chicago is self-confident. He
can guess at least why in old communities, like
Hardy's Wessex or the North of France, the inhabitants
of villages not ten miles apart will differ in temperament and often in temper, hill town varying from
lowland village beneath it sometimes more than Kansas City from Minneapolis. He knows that the old
elemental forces—wind, water, fire, and earth—still
mold men's thoughts and lives a hundred times more
than they guess, even when pavements, electric lights,
tight roofs, and artificial heat seem to make nature
only a name. He knows that the sights and sounds
and smells about us, clouds, songs, and wind murmur-
ings, rain-washed earth, and fruit trees blossoming, enter into our sub-consciousness with a power but seldom
appraised. Prison life, factory service long continued,
a clerk's stool, a housewife's day-long duties—these
things stunt and transform the human animal as nothing else, because of all experiences they most restrict,
most impoverish the natural environment. And it is
the especial function of nature books to make vivid
and warm and sympathetic our background of nature.
They make conscious our sub-conscious dependence
upon earth that bore us. They do not merely inform

(there the scientist may transcend them), they enrich the subtle relationship between us and our environment. Move a civilization and its literature from one hemisphere to another, and their adapting, adjusting services become most valuable. Men like Thoreau are worth more than we have ever guessed.

No one has ever written more honest books than Thoreau's "Walden," his "Autumn," "Summer," and the rest. There is not one literary flourish in the whole of them, although they are done with consummate literary care; nothing but honest, if not always accurate, observation of the world of hill-slopes, waves, flowers, birds, and beasts, and honest, shrewd philosophizing as to what it all meant for him, an American. Here is a man content to take a walk, fill his mind with observation, and then come home to think. Repeat the walk, repeat or vary the observation, change or expand the thought, and you have Thoreau. No wonder he brought his first edition home, not seriously depleted, and made his library of it! Thoreau needs excerpting to be popular. Most nature books do. But not to be valuable!

For see what this queer genius was doing. Lovingly, laboriously, and sometimes a little tediously, he was studying his environment. For some generations his ancestors had lived on a new soil, too busy in squeezing life from it to be practically aware of its differences. They and the rest had altered Massachusetts. Massachusetts had altered them. Why? To what? The answer is not yet ready. But here is one descendant who will know at least what Massachusetts *is*—wave, wind, soil, and the life therein and thereon. He begins humbly with the little things; but humanly, not as the out-and-out scientist goes to work, to classify or to study the narrower laws of organic development; or romantically as the sentimentalist, who intones his "Ah!" at the sight of dying leaves or the cocoon becoming moth. It is all human, and yet all intensely practical with Thoreau. He envies the Indian not because he is "wild," or "free," or any such nonsense, but for his instinctive adaptations to his background,—because nature has become traditional, stimulative with him. And simply, almost naïvely, he sets down what he has discovered. The land I live in is like this or that; such and such life lives in it; and this is what it all means for me, the transplanted European, for us, Americans, who have souls to shape and characters to mold in a new environment, under influences subtler than we guess. "I make it my business to extract from Nature whatever nutriment she can furnish me, though at the risk of endless iteration. I milk the sky and the earth." And again: "Surely it is a defect in our Bible that it is not truly ours, but a Hebrew Bible. The most pertinent illustrations for us are to be drawn not from Egypt or Babylonia, but from New England. Natural objects and phenomena are the original symbols or types which express our thoughts and feelings. Yet American scholars, having little or no root in the soil, commonly strive with all their might to confine themselves to the imported symbols alone. All the true growth and experience, the living speech, they would fain reject as 'Americanisms.' It is the old error which the church, the state, the school, ever commit, choosing darkness rather than light, holding fast to the old and to tradition. When I really know that our river pursues a serpentine course to the Merrimac, shall I continue to describe it by referring to some other river, no older than itself, which is like it, and call it a meander? It is no more meandering than the Meander is musketaquiding."

This for Thoreau was going back to nature. Our historians of literature who cite him as an example of how to be American without being strenuous, as an instance of leisure nobly earned, are quite wrong. If any man has striven to make us at home in America, it is Thoreau. He gave his life to it; and in some measure it is thanks to him that with most Americans you reach intimacy most quickly by talking about "the woods."

Thoreau gave to this American tendency the touch of genius and the depth of real thought. After his day the "back-to-nature" idea became more popular and perhaps more picturesque. Our literature becomes more and more aware of an American background. Bobolinks and thrushes take the place of skylarks; sumach and cedar begin to be as familiar as heather and gorse; forests, prairies, a clear, high sky, a snowy winter, a summer of thunderstorms, drive out the misty England which, since the days of Cynewulf, our ancestors had seen in the mind's eye while they were writing. Nature literature becomes a category. Men make their reputations by means of it.

No one has yet catalogued—so far as I am aware —the vast collection of back-to-nature books that followed Thoreau. No one has ever seriously criticized it, except Mr. Roosevelt, who with characteristic vigor of phrase, stamped "nature-faking" on its worser half. But every one reads in it. Indeed, the popularity of such writing has been so great as to make us distrust its serious literary value. And yet, viewed internationally, there are few achievements in American literature so original. I will not say that John Muir and John Burroughs, upon whom Thoreau's mantle fell, have written great books. Probably not. Certainly it is too soon to say. But when you have gathered the names of Gilbert White, Jeffries, Fabre, Maeterlinck, and in slightly different *genres,* Izaak Walton, Hudson, and Kipling from various literatures you will find few others abroad to list with ours. Nor do our men owe one jot or tittle of their inspiration to individuals on the other side of the water.

Locally, too, these books are more noteworthy than may at first appear. They are curiously passionate, and passion in American literature since the Civil War is rare. I do not mean sentiment, or romance, or eroticism. I mean such passion as Wordsworth felt for his lakes, Byron (even when most Byronic) for the ocean, the author of "The Song of Roland" for his Franks. Muir loved the Yosemite as a man might love a woman. Every word he wrote of the Sierras is touched with intensity. Hear him after a day on Alaskan peaks: "Dancing down the mountain to camp, my mind glowing like the sunbeaten glaciers, I found the Indians seated around a good fire, entirely happy now that the farthest point of the journey was safely reached and the long, dark storm was cleared away. How hopefully, peacefully bright that night were the stars in the frosty sky, and how impressive was the thunder of icebergs, rolling, swelling, reverberating through the solemn stillness! I was too happy to sleep."

Such passion, and often such style, is to be found in all these books when they are good books. Compare a paragraph or two of the early Burroughs on his birch-clad lake country, or Thoreau upon Concord pines, with the "natural history paragraph" that English magazines used to publish, and you will feel it. Compare any of the lesser nature books of the mid-nineteenth century—Clarence King's "Mountaineering in the Sierras," for example—with the current novel writing of the period and you will feel the greater sincerity. A passion for nature! Except the New England passion for ideals, Whitman's passion for democracy, and Poe's lonely devotion to beauty, I sometimes think that this is the only great passion that has found its way into American literature.

Hence the "nature fakers." The passion of one generation becomes the sentiment of the next. And sentiment is easily capitalized. The individual can be stirred by nature as she is. A hermit thrush singing in moonlight above a Catskill clove will move him. But the populace will require something more sensational. To the sparkling water of truth must be added the syrup of sentiment and the cream of romance. Mr. Kipling, following ancient traditions of the Orient, gave personalities to his animals so that stories might be made from them. Mr. Long, Mr. Roberts, Mr. London, Mr. Thompson-Seton, and the rest, have told stories about animals so that the American interest in nature might be exploited. The difference is essential. If the "Jungle Books" teach anything it is the moral ideals of the British Empire. But our nature romancers—a fairer term than "fakers," since they do not willingly "fake"—teach the background and tradition of our soil. In the process they inject sentiment, giving us the noble desperation of the stag, the startling wolf-longings of the dog, and the picturesque outlawry of the ground hog,—and get a hundred readers where Thoreau got one.

This is the same indictment as that so often brought against the stock American novel, that it prefers the gloss of easy sentiment to the rough, true fact, that it does not grapple direct with things as they are in America, but looks at them through optimist's glasses that obscure and soften the scene. Nevertheless, I very much prefer the sentimentalized animal story to the sentimentalized man story. The first, as narrative, may be romantic bosh, but it does give one a loving, faithful study of background that is worth the price that it costs in illusion. It reaches my emotions as a novelist who splashed his sentiment with equal profusion never could. My share of the race mind is willing even to be tricked into sympathy with its environment. I would rather believe that the sparrow on my telephone wire is swearing at the robin on my lawn than never to notice either of them!

How curiously complete and effective is the service of these nature books, when all is considered. There is no better instance, I imagine, of how literature and life act and react upon one another. The plain American takes to the woods because he wants to, he does not know why. The writing American puts the woods into his books, also because he wants to, although I suspect that sometimes he knows very well why. Nevertheless, the same general tendency, the same impulse, lie behind both. But reading nature books makes us crave more nature, and every gratification of curiosity marks itself upon the sub-consciousness. Thus the clear, vigorous tradition of the soil passes through us to our books, and from our books to us. It is the soundest, the sweetest, if not the greatest and deepest inspiration of American literature. In the confusion that attends the meeting here of all the races it is something to cling to; it is our own.

Thanks to the Artists

It would be a wise American town that gave up paying "boosters" and began to support its artists. A country is just so much country until it has been talked about, painted, or put into literature. A town is just so many brick and wood squares, inhabited by human animals, until some one's creative and interpretative mind has given it "atmosphere," by which we mean significance.

America was not mere wild land to the early colonists: it was a country that had already been seen through the eyes of enthusiastic explorers and daring adventurers, whose airs were sweeter than Europe's, whose fruits were richer, where forest and game, and even the savage inhabitant, guaranteed a more exciting life, full of chance for the future.

New England was not just so much stony acre and fishing village for the men of the 'twenties and 'forties. It was a land haloed by the hopes and sufferings of forefathers, where every town had its record of struggle known to all by word of mouth or book.

And when the New Englanders pushed westward, it was to a wilderness which already had its literature, along trails of which they had read, and into regions familiar to them in imagination.

Say what you please, and it is easy to say too much, of the imitativeness of American literature as Irving,

Cooper, Hawthorne, Longfellow, Thoreau, Twain, and
Howells wrote it, nevertheless, it was more than justified by the human significance it gave to mere land
in America; and it is richer and more valuable than
much later writing just because of this attempt. Without Hawthorne and Thoreau, New England would have
lost its past; without Cooper and Parkman the word
"frontier" would mean no more than "boundary" to
most of us.

It is foolish to lay a burden on art, and to say, for
example, that American novelists must accept the same
obligation to cities and country to-day. But we may
justly praise and thank them when they do enrich
this somewhat monotonous America that has been
planed over by the movies, the *Saturday Evening Post,*
quick transportation, and the newspaper with its syndi-
cated features, until it is as repetitive as a tom-tom.

After the Civil War every one began to move in
America, and the immigrants, moving in, moved also,
so that roots were pulled up everywhere and the town
one lived in became as impersonal as a hotel, the farm
no more human than a seed-bed. Literature of the
time shows this in two ways: the rarity of books that
give a local habitation and a name to the familiar,
contemporary scene; and a romantic interest, as of the
half-starved, in local color stories of remote districts
where history and tradition still meant something in
the lives of the inhabitants.

It is encouraging to see how rapidly all this is changing. In poetry the Middle West and New England

have been made again to figure in the imagination. Rural New Hampshire and Illinois are alive to-day for those who have read Masters, Lindsay, and Frost. In prose Chicago, New York, New Haven, Richmond, Detroit, San Francisco, and the ubiquitous Main Street of a hundred Gopher Prairies have become wayfares for the memory of the reader, as well as congeries of amusement and trade. In particular our universities, which in the 'eighties and 'nineties were darkly lit by a few flaring torches of mawkish romance, have been illumined for the imagination by a series of stories that already begin to make the undergraduate comprehend his place in one of the richest streams of history, and graduates to understand their youth. Poole's "The Harbor" (which served both college and city), Owen Johnson's "Stover at Yale," Norris's "Salt," Fitzgerald's "This Side of Paradise," Stephen Benét's "The Beginning of Wisdom"—these books and many others have, like the opening chapters of Compton Mackenzie's English "Sinister Street," given depth, color, and significance to the college, which may not increase its immediate and measurable efficiency but certainly strengthen its grip upon the imagination, and therefore upon life.

Planners, builders, laborers, schemers, executives make a city, a county, a university habitable, give them their bones and their blood. Poets and novelists make us appreciate the life we live in them, give them their souls. The best "boosters" are artists, because their boosting lasts.

To-day in American Literature: Addressed to the British *

THE analysis of conditions and tendencies in contemporary American literature which I wish to present in this lecture, requires historical background, detailed criticism, and a study of development. I have time for reference to none of these, and can only summarize the end of the process. If, therefore, I seem to generalize unduly, I hope that my deficiencies may be charged against the exigencies of the occasion. But I generalize the more boldly because I am speaking, after all, of an English literature; not in a Roman-Greek relationship of unnaturalized borrowings (for we Americans imitate less and less), but English by common cultural inheritance, by identical language, and by deeply resembling character. Nevertheless, the more American literature diverges from British (and that divergence is already wide) the more truly English, the less colonial does it become. A Briton should not take unkindly assertions of independence, even such ruffled independence as Lowell expressed in "The Biglow Papers":

* This lecture was, in fact, delivered in the summer of 1918 at Cambridge University as part of a summer session devoted to the United States of America. It is reprinted in lecture form in order that the point of view may carry its own explanation.

I guess the Lord druv down Creation's spiles
'Thout no *gret* helpin' from the British Isles,
An' could contrive to keep things pooty stiff
Ef they withdrawed from business in a miff;
I han't no patience with such swelling fellers ez
Think God can't forge 'thout them to blow the bellerses.

I desire neither to apologize for American literature, nor to boast of it. No apology is necessary now, whatever Sydney Smith may have thought in earlier days: and it is decidedly not the time to boast, for so far literature has usually been a by-product in the development of American aptitudes. But it may be useful to state broadly at the beginning some of the difficulties and the closely related advantages that condition the making of literature in the United States.

The critic of American literature usually begins in this fashion: America, in somewhat over a century, has built up a political and social organization admittedly great. She has not produced, however, a great literature: great writers she has produced, but not a great literature. The reason is, that so much energy has been employed in developing the resources of a great country, that little has been left to expend in creative imagination. The currents of genius have flowed toward trade, agriculture, and manufacturing, not esthetics.

This explanation is easy to understand, and is therefore plausible, but I do not believe that it is accurate. It is not true that American energy has been absorbed by business. Politics, and politics of a creative character, has never lacked good blood in the United States. Organization, and organization of a kind requiring the creative intellect, has drawn enormously upon our energies, especially since the Civil War, and by no means all of it has been business organization. Consider our systems of education and philanthropy, erected for vast needs. And I venture to guess that more varieties of religious experience have arisen in America than elsewhere in the same period. After all, why expect a century and a half of semi-independent intellectual existence to result in a great national literature? Can other countries, other times, show such a phenomenon?

No, if we have been slow in finding ourselves in literature, in creating a school of expression like the Elizabethan or the Augustan, the difficulties are to be sought elsewhere than in a lack of energy.

Seek them first of all in a weakening of literary tradition. The sky changes, not the mind, said Horace, but this is true only of the essentials of being. The great writers of our common English tradition— Chaucer, Shakespeare, Milton, and many others—are as good for us as they are good for you. It is even whispered that our language is more faithful to their diction than is yours. But the conditions of life in a new environment bring a multitude of minor changes with them. To begin with little things, our climate, our birds, our trees, our daily contact with nature, are all different. Your mellow fluting blackbird, your wise thrush that sings each song twice over, your high-fluttering larks we do not know. Our blackbird creaks discordantly, our plaintive lark sings from the meadow tussock, our thrush chimes his heavenly bell from forest dimness. And this accounts, may I suggest in passing, for the insistence upon nature in American writing, from Thoreau down. Our social and economic experience has been widely different also; and all this, plus the results of a break in space and time with the home country of our language, weakened that traditional influence which is so essential for the production of a national literature. It had to be; good will come of it; but for a time we vacillated, and we still vacillate, like a new satellite finding its course.

Again, the constant shift of location within America has been a strong delaying factor. Moving-day has come at least once a generation for most American families since the days of William Penn or *The Mayflower*. The president of a Western university, who himself, as a baby, had been carried across the Alleghenies in a sling, once told me the history of his family. It settled in Virginia in the seventeenth century, and moved westward regularly each generation, until his father, the sixth or seventh in line, had reached California. On the return journey he had got as far as Illinois, and his son was moving to New York! The disturbing effect upon literature of this constant change of soils and environment is best proved by negatives. Wherever there has been a settled community in the United States—in New England of the 'forties and again in the 'nineties, in the Middle West and California to-day—one is sure to find a literature with some depth and solidity to it. The New England civilization of the early nineteenth century, now materially altered, was a definable culture, with five generations behind it, and strong roots in the old world. From it came the most mature school of American literature that so far we have possessed.

Still another difficulty must be added. The social. Pessimists, who see in our Eastern states a mere congeries of all the white races, and some not white, bewail the impossibility of a real nation in America. But the racial problem has always been with us, nor has it by any means always been unsolved. Before the Revolution, we were English, Scottish, Welsh, Low German, Huguenot, Dutch, and Swedish. Before the Civil War, we were the same plus the Irish and the Germans of '48. And now we add Slavs, Jews, Greeks, and Italians. I do not minimize the danger. But let it be understood that while our civilization has always been British (if that term is used in its broadest sense) our blood has always been mixed, even in Virginia and New England. This has made it hard for us to feel entirely at home in the only literary tradition we possessed and cared to possess. We have been like the man with a ready-made suit. The cloth is right, but the cut must be altered before the clothes will fit him.

And finally, America has always been decentralized intellectually. It is true that most of the books and magazines are published in New York, and have always been published there, or in Boston or Philadelphia. But they have been written all over a vast country by men and women who frequently never see each other in the flesh. There has been no center like London, where writers can rub elbows half-a-dozen times a year. Boston was such a capital once; only, however, for New England. New York is a clearing-house of literature now; but the writing is, most of it, done elsewhere. It is curious to speculate what might have happened if the capital of the United States had been fixed at New York instead of Washington!

From this decentralization there results a lack of literary self-confidence that is one of the most important factors in the intellectual life of America. The writer in Tucson or Minneapolis or Bangor is dependent upon his neighbors to a degree impossible in Manchester or Glasgow or York. He is marooned there, separated in space and time, if not in mind, from men and women who believe, as he may believe, in the worth of literary standards, in the necessity of making not the most easily readable book, but the best. Here is one cause of the feebleness of many American "literary" books.

Nevertheless, this very decentralization may have, when we reach literary maturity, its great advantages. It is difficult to over-estimate the color, the variety, the *verve* of American life. And much of this comes not from the push and "hustle" and energy of America —for energy is just energy all the world over—but is rather to be found in the new adjustments of race and environment which are multiplying infinitely all over the United States. It is true that American civilization seems to be monotonous—that one sees the same magazines and books, the same moving-picture shows, the same drug-stores, trolley cars, and hotels on a New York model, hears the same slang and much the same general conversation from New Haven to Los Angeles. But this monotony is superficial. Beneath the surface there are infinite strainings and divergences —the peasant immigrant working toward, the well-established provincial holding to, the wide-ranging mind of the intellectual working away from, this dead level of conventional standards. Where we are going, it is not yet possible to say. Quite certainly not toward an un-British culture. Most certainly not toward a culture merely neo-English. But in any case, it is because San Francisco and Indianapolis and Chicago and Philadelphia have literary republics of their own, sovereign like our states, yet highly federalized also in a common bond of American taste and ideals which the war made stronger—it is this fact that makes it possible to record, as American writers are already recording, the multifarious, confused development of racial instincts working into a national consciousness. Localization is our difficulty; it is also the only means by which literature can keep touch with life in so huge a congeries as America. If we can escape provincialism and yet remain local, all will be well.

So far I have been merely defining the terms upon which literature has been written in America. Let me add to these terms a classification. If one stretches the meaning of literature to cover all writing in prose or verse that is not simply informative, then four categories will include all literary writing in America that is in any way significant. We have an artistocratic and a democratic literature; we have a dilettante and a vast bourgeois literature.

In using the term aristocratic literature I have in mind an intellectual rather than a social category. I mean all writing addressed to specially trained intelligence, essays that imply a rich background of knowledge and taste, stories dependent upon psychological analysis, poetry which is austere in content or complex in form. I mean Henry James and Sherwood Anderson, Mr. Cabell, Mr. Hergesheimer, and Mrs. Wharton, Agnes Repplier, Mr. Crothers, Mr. Sherman, and Mr. Colby.

By democratic literature I mean all honest writing, whether crude or carefully wrought, that endeavors to interpret the American scene in typical aspects for all who care to read. I mean Walt Whitman and Edgar Lee Masters; I mean a hundred writers of short stories who, lacking perhaps the final touch of art, have nevertheless put a new world and a new people momentarily upon the stage. I mean the addresses of Lincoln and of President Wilson.

With dilettante literature I come to a very different and less important classification: the vast company—how vast few even among natives suspect—of would-be writers, who in every town and county of the United States are writing, writing, writing what they hope to be literature, what is usually but a pallid imitation of worn-out literary forms. More people seem to be engaged in occasional production of poetry and fiction—and especially of poetry—in America, than in any single money-making enterprise characteristic of a great industrial nation. The flood pours through every editorial office in the land, trickles into the corners of country newspapers, makes short-lived dilettante magazines, and runs back, most of it, to its makers. It is not literature, for the bulk is bloodless, sentimental, or cheap, but it is significant of the now passionate American desire to express our nascent soul.

My chief difficulty is to explain what I mean by bourgeois literature. The flood of dilettante writing is subterranean; it is bourgeois literature that makes the visible rivers and oceans of American writing. And these fluid areas are like the lakes on maps of Central Asia—bounds cannot be set to them. One finds magazines (and pray remember that the magazine is as great a literary force as the book in America), one finds magazines whose entire function is to be admirably bourgeois for their two million odd of readers. And in the more truly literary and "aristocratic" periodicals, in the books published for the discriminating, the bourgeois creeps in and often is dominant. The bourgeois in American literature is a special variety that must not be too quickly identified with the literary product that bears the same name in more static civilizations. It is nearly always clever. Witness our short stories, which even when calculated not to puzzle the least intelligence nor to transcend the most modest limitations of taste, must be carefully constructed and told with facility or they will never see the light. And this literature is nearly always true to the superficies of life, to which, indeed, it confines itself. Wild melodrama is more and more being relegated to the "movies," soft sentimentality still has its place in the novel, but is losing ground in the people's library, the magazines. Life as the American believes he is living it, is the subject of bourgeois literature. But the sad limitation upon this vast output is that, whether poetry, criticism, or fiction, it does not interpret, it merely pictures; and this is the inevitable failure of pages that must be written always for a million or more of readers. It is standardized literature; and good literature, like the best airplanes, cannot be standardized.

Now the error made by most English critics in endeavoring to estimate the potentialities or the actualities of American literature, is to judge under the influence of this crushing weight of clever, mediocre writing. They feel, quite justly, its enormous energy and its terrible cramping power. They see that the best of our democratic writers belong on its fringe; see also that our makers of aristocratic literature and our dilettante escape its weight only when they cut themselves off from the life beat of the nation. And therefore, as a distinguished English poet recently said, America is doomed to a hopeless and ever-spreading mediocrity.

With this view I wish to take immediate issue upon grounds that are both actual and theoretical. There is a fallacy here to begin with, a fallacious analogy. It is true, I believe, in Great Britain, and also in France, that there are two separate publics; that the readers who purchase from the news stands are often as completely unaware of literary books for literary people as if these bore the imprint of the moon. But even in England the distinction is by no means sharp; and in America it is not a question of distinctions at all, but of gradations. In our better magazines are to be found all the categories of which I have written—even the dilettante; and it is a bold critic who will assert that pages one to twenty are read only by one group, and pages twenty to forty only by another. We are the most careless readers in the world; but also the most voracious and the most catholic.

And next, let us make up our minds once for all that a bourgeois literature—by which, let me repeat, I mean a literature that is good without being very good, true without being utterly true, clever without being fine—is a necessity for a vast population moving upward from generation to generation in the intellectual scale, toward a level that must be relatively low in order to be attainable. Let us say that such a literature cannot be real literature. I am content with that statement. But it must exist, and good may come of it.

This is the critical point toward which I have been moving in this lecture, and it is here that the hopeful influence of the American spirit, as I interpret it to-day, assumes its importance. That spirit is both idealistic and democratic. Idealistic in the sense that there is a profound and often foolishly optimistic belief in America that every son can be better than his father, better in education, better in taste, better in the power to accomplish and understand. Democratic in this sense, that with less political democracy than one finds in Great Britain, there is again a fundamental belief that every tendency, every taste, every capacity, like every man, should have its chance somehow, somewhere, to get a hearing, to secure its deservings, to make, to have, to learn what seems the best.

A vague desire, you say, resulting in confusion and mediocrity. This is true and will be true for some time longer; but instead of arguing in generalities let me illustrate these results by the literature I have been discussing.

When brought to bear upon the category of the dilettante, it is precisely this desire for "general improvement" that has encouraged such a curious outpouring from mediocre though sensitive hearts. The absence of strong literary tradition, the lack of deep literary soil, has been responsible for the insipidity of the product. The habit of reference to the taste of the majority has prevented us from taking this product too seriously. Without that instinctive distrust of the merely literary common to all bourgeois communities, we might well be presenting to you as typical American literature a gentle weakling whose manners, when he has them, have been formed abroad.

Aristocratic literature has suffered in one respect from the restraints of democracy and the compulsions of democratic idealism. It has lacked the self-confidence and therefore the vigor of its parallels in the old world. Emerson and Thoreau rose above these restrictions, and so did Hawthorne and Poe. But in later generations especially, our intellectual poetry and intellectual prose is too frequently though by no means always less excellent than yours. Nevertheless, thanks to the influence of this bourgeois spirit upon the intellects that in American towns must live with, if not share it; thanks, also, to the magazines through which our finer minds must appeal to the public rather than to a circle or a clique, the nerves of transfer between the community at large and the intellectuals are active, the tendons that unite them strong. I argue much from this.

Now theoretically, where you find an instinctive and therefore an honest passion for the ideals of democracy, you should find a great literature expressing and interpreting the democracy. I have given already some reasons why in practice this has not yet become an actuality in America. Let me add, in discussing the bearing of this argument upon the third category of American literature, the democratic, one more.

I doubt whether we yet know precisely what is meant by a great democratic literature. Democracy has been in transition at least since the French Revolution; it is in rapid transition now. The works which we call democratic are many of them expressive of phases merely of the popular life, just as so much American literature is expressive of localities and groups in America.

And usually the works of genius that we do possess have been written by converted aristocrats, like Tolstoy, and have a little of the fanaticism and over-emphasis of the convert. Or they represent and share the turgidity of the minds they interpret, like some of the work of Walt Whitman. All this is true, and yet a careful reader of American literature must be more impressed by such prose as Lincoln's, by such poems as Whitman's, such fiction as Mark Twain's at his best, than by many more elegant works of polite literature. For these—and I could add to them dozens of later stories and poems, ephemeral perhaps but showing what may be done when we burst the bourgeois chain —for these are discoveries in the vigor, the poignancy, the color of our democratic national life.

I have already hinted at what seems to me the way out and up for American literature. It will not be by fine writing that borrows or adapts foreign models, even English models which are not foreign to us. It will not come through geniuses of the backwoods, adopted by some coterie, and succeeding, when they do succeed, by their strangeness rather than the value of the life they depict. That might have happened in the romantic decades of the early nineteenth century; but our English literary tradition was a saving influence which kept us from *gaucherie,* even if it set limits upon our strength. Our expectation, so I think, is in the slowly mounting level of the vast bourgeois literature that fills not excellently, but certainly not discreditably, our books and magazines. There, and not in coteries, is our school of writing. When originality wearies of stereotypes and conventions, when energy and ability force the editorial hand, and appeal to the desire of Americans to know themselves, we shall begin a new era in American literature. Our problem is not chiefly to expose and attack and discredit the flat conventionality of popular writing. It is rather to crack the smooth and monotonous surface and stir the fire beneath it, until the lava of new and true imaginings can pour through. And this is, historically, the probable course of evolution. It was the Elizabethan fashion. The popular forms took life and fire then. The advice of the classicists, who wished to ignore the crude drama beloved of the public, was not heeded; it will not be heeded now. Our task is to make a bourgeois democracy fruitful. We must work with what we have.

Much has been said of the advantage for us, and perhaps for the world, which has come from the separation of the American colonies from Great Britain. Two systems of closely related political thinking, two national characters, have developed and been successful instead of one. Your ancestors opened the door of departure for mine, somewhat brusquely it is true, but with the same result, if not the same reason, as with the boys they sent away to school—they made men of us.

So it is with literature. American literature will never, as some critics would persuade us, be a child without a parent. In its fundamental character it is, and will remain, British, because at bottom the American character, whatever its blood mixture, is formed upon customs and ideals that have the same origin and a parallel development with yours. But this literature, like our political institutions, will not duplicate; like the seedling, it will make another tree and not another branch. In literature we are still pioneers. I think that it may be reserved for us to discover a literature for the new democracy of English-speaking peoples that is coming—a literature for the common people who do not wish to stay common. Like Lincoln's, it will not be vulgar; like Whitman's, never tawdry; like Mark Twain's, not empty of penetrating thought; like Shakespeare's it will be popular. If this should happen, as I believe it may, it would be a just return upon our share of a great inheritance.

Time's Mirror

WHAT is the use of criticizing modern literature unless you are willing to criticize modern life? And how many Americans are willing to criticize it with eyes wide open?

The outstanding fact in mass civilization as it exists in America and Western Europe to-day is that it moves with confidence in only one direction. The workers, after their escape from the industrial slavery of the last century, have only one plan for the future upon which they can unite, a greater share in material benefits. The possessors of capital have only one program upon which they agree, a further exploitation of material resources, for the greater comfort of the community and themselves. The professional classes have only one professional instinct in common, to discover new methods by which man's comfort may be made secure.

In this way of life, as the Buddhist might have called it, all our really effective energy discharges itself. Even the church is most active in social service, and philosophy is accounted most original when it accounts for behavior. Theology has become a stagnant science, and, to prove the rule by contraries, the main problem of man's spiritual relation to the universe, his end in liv-

ing, and the secret of real happiness is left to a sentimental idealism in which reason, as the Greeks knew
it, has less and less place, and primitive instinct, as the
anthropologists define it, and the Freudian psychologists explain it, is given more and more control.

The flat truth is that, as a civilization, we are less
sure of where we are going, where we want to go, how
and for what we wish to live, than at any intelligent
period of which we have full record. This is not pessimism. It is merely a fact, which is dependent upon
our failure to digest the problems that democracy, machinery, feminism, and the destruction of our working
dogmas by scientific discovery, have presented to us.
All these things are more likely to be good than bad,
all bear promise for the future, but all tend to confuse
contemporary men. New power over nature has been
given them and they are engaged in seizing it. New
means of testing preconceived opinion are theirs, and
they are using them. The numbers which can be called
intelligent are tremendously augmented and the race to
secure material comforts has become a mass movement which will not cease until the objective is won.

In the meantime, there is only one road which is
clear—the road of material progress, and whether its
end lies in the new barbarism of a mechanistic state
where the mental and physical faculties will decline in
proportion to the means discovered for healing their
ills, or whether it is merely a path where the privileged
leaders must mark step for a while until the unpriv-
ileged masses catch up with them in material welfare,

no one knows and few that are really competent care to inquire.

Now this obsession with material welfare is the underlying premise with which all discussion of contemporary literature, and particularly American literature, must begin. Ours is a literature of an age without dogma, which is to say without a theory of living; the literature of an inductive, an experimental period, where the really vital attempt is to subdue physical environment (for the first time in history) to the needs of the common man. It is an age, therefore, interested and legitimately interested in behavior rather than character, in matter and its laws rather than in the control of matter for the purposes of fine living.

Therefore, our vital literature is behavioristic, naturalistic, experimental—rightly so I think—and must be so until we seek another way. That search cannot be long deferred. One expects its beginning at any moment, precisely as one expects, and with reason, a reaction against the lawless thinking and unrestrained impulses which have followed the war. One hopes that it will not be to Puritanism, unless it be that stoic state of mind which lay behind Puritanism, for no old solution will serve. The neo-Puritans to-day abuse the rebels, young and old, because they have thrown over dogma and discipline. The rebels accuse Puritanism for preserving the dogma that cramps instead of frees. It is neither return to the old nor the destruction thereof that we must seek, but a new religion, a new discipline, a new hope, and a new end which can give more significance to living than dwellers in our industrial civilization are now finding.

In the meantime, those who seek literary consolation are by no means to be urged away from their own literature, which contains a perfect picture of our feverish times, and has implicit within it the medicine for our ills, if they are curable. But they may be advised to go again and more often than is now the fashion to the writings of those men who found for their own time, a real significance, who could formulate a saving doctrine, and who could give to literature what it chiefly lacks to-day, a core of ethical conviction and a view of man in his world *sub specie æternitatis*. It is the appointed time in which to read Dante and Milton, Shakespeare, and Goethe, above all Plato and the great tragedies of Greece. Our laughter would be sweeter if there were more depth of thought and emotion to our serious moods.

The Family Magazine

READERS who like magazines will be pleased, those who do not like them perhaps distressed, to learn, if they are not already aware of it, that the magazine as we know it to-day is distinctly an American creation. They may stir, or soothe, their aroused emotions by considering that the magazine which began in England literally as a storehouse of miscellanies attained in mid-nineteenth century United States a dignity, a harmony, and a format which gave it preëminence among periodicals. *Harper's* and *The Century* in particular shared with Mark Twain and the sewing machine the honor of making America familiarly known abroad.

I do not wish to overburden this essay with history, but one of the reasons for the appearance of such a dominating medium in a comparatively unliterary country is relevant to the discussion to follow. The magazine of those days was vigorous. It was vigorous because, unlike other American publications, it was not oppressed by competition. Until the laws of international copyright were completed, the latest novels of the Victorians, then at their prime, could be rushed from a steamer, and distributed in editions which were cheap because no royalties had to be paid. Thackeray and Dickens could be sold at a discount, where American authors of less reputation had to meet full charges. And the like was true of poetry. But the magazine, like the newspaper, was not international; it was national at least in its entirety, and for it British periodicals could not be substituted. Furthermore, it could, and did, especially in its earlier years, steal unmercifully from England, so that a subscriber got both homebrew and imported for a single payment. Thus the magazine flourished in the mid-century while the American novel declined.

A notable instance of this vigor was the effect of the growing magazine upon the infant short story. Our American magazine made the development of the American short story possible by creating a need for good short fiction. The rise of our short story, after a transitional period when the earliest periodicals and the illustrated Annuals sought good short stories and could not get them, coincides with the rise of the family magazine. It was such a demand that called forth the powers in prose of the poet, Poe. And as our magazine has become the best of its kind, so in the short story, and in the short story alone, does American literature rival the more fecund literatures of England and Europe.

That a strong and native tendency made the American magazine is indicated by the effect of our atmosphere upon the periodical which the English have always called a review. Import that form, as was done for *The North American, The Atlantic Monthly, The Forum,* or *The Yale Review,* and immediately the new

American periodical begins to be a little more of a magazine, a little more miscellaneous in its content, a little less of a critical survey. Critical articles give place to memoirs and sketches, fiction or near fiction creeps in. There is always a tendency to lose type and be absorbed into the form that the mid-century had made so successful: a periodical, handsomely illustrated, with much fiction, some description, a little serious comment on affairs written for the general reader, occasional poetry, and enough humor to guarantee diversion. This is our national medium for literary expression—an admirable medium for a nation of long-distance commuters. And it is this "family magazine" I wish to discuss in its literary aspects.

The dominance of the family magazine as a purveyor of general literature in America has continued, but in our own time the species (like other strong organisms) has divided into two genres, which are more different than, on the surface, they appear. The illustrated *literary* magazine (the family magazine *par excellence*) must now be differentiated from the illustrated *journalistic* magazine, but both are as American in origin as the review and the critical weekly are English.

It was the native vigor of the family magazine that led to the Great Divergence of the 'nineties, which older readers will remember well. The literary historian of that period usually gives a different explanation. He is accustomed to say that the old-time "quality" magazines, *Harper's, Scribner's,* and the rest, were growing moribund when, by an effort of editorial genius, Mr. McClure created a new and rebellious type of magazine, which was rapidly imitated. We called it, as I remember, for want of a better title, the fifteen-cent magazine. In the wake of *McClure's*, came *Collier's*, *The Saturday Evening Post*, *The Ladies Home Journal*, and all the long and profitable train which adapted the McClurean discovery to special needs and circumstances.

I do not believe that this is a true statement of what happened in the fruitful 'nineties. *McClure's* was not, speaking biologically, a new species at all; it was only a mutation in which the recessive traits of the old magazine became dominant while the invaluable type was preserved. To speak more plainly, the literary magazine, as America knew it, had always printed news, matured news, often stale news, but still journalism. Read any number of *Harper's* in the 'seventies for proof. And, *pari passu*, American journalism was eagerly trying to discover some outlet for its finer products, a medium where good pictures, sober afterthoughts, and the finish that comes from careful writing were possible. *Harper's Weekly* in Civil War days, and later, was its creation.

And now it was happily discovered that the family magazine had a potential popularity far greater than its limited circulation. With its month-long period of incubation, its elastic form, in which story, special article, poetry, picture, humor, could all be harmoniously combined, only a redistribution of emphasis was necessary in order to make broader its appeal. Mr. McClure journalized the family magazine. He introduced financial and economic news in the form of sensational investigations, he bid for stories more lively, more immediate in their interest, more journalistic than we were accustomed to read (Kipling's journalistic stories for example, were first published in America in *Mc-Clure's*). He accepted pictures in which certainty of hitting the public eye was substituted for a guarantee of art. And yet, with a month to prepare his number, and only twelve issues a year, he could pay for excellence, and insure it, as no newspaper had ever been able to do. And he was freed from the incubus of "local news" and day-by-day reports. In brief, under his midwifery, the literary magazine gave birth to a super-newspaper.

Needless to say, the great increase in the number of American readers and the corresponding decline in the average intelligence and discrimination of the reading public had much to do with the success of the journalistic magazine. Yet it may be stated, with equal truth, that the rapid advance in the average intelligence of the American public as a whole made a market for a super-newspaper in which nothing was hurried and everything well done. The contributions to literature through this new journalism have been at least as great during the period of its existence as from the "quality" magazine, the contributions toward the support of American authors much greater. Like all good journalism, it has included real literature when it could get and "get away with it."

Birth, however, in the literary as in the animal world, is exhausting and often leaves the parent in a debility which may lead to death. The periodical essay of the eighteenth century bore the novel of character, and died; the Gothic tale of a later date perished of the short story to which it gave its heart blood. The family magazine of the literary order has been debile, so radical critics charge, since its journalistic offspring began to sweep America. Shall it die?

By no means. An America without the illustrated literary magazine, dignified, respectable, certain to contain something that a reader of taste can peruse with pleasure, would be an unfamiliar America. And it would be a barer America. In spite of our brood of special magazines for the *literati* and the advanced, which Mr. Ford Madox Hueffer praises so warmly, we are not so well provided with the distributive machinery for a national culture as to flout a recognized agency with a gesture and a sneer. But the family magazine has undeniably lost its vigorous appeal, and must be reinvigorated. The malady is due to no slackening of literary virility in the country; indeed there has probably not been so much literary energy in the country since the 'forties as now—not nearly so much. Nor is it due to a lack of good readers. Nor, in my opinion, to the competition of the journalistic magazine. The literary magazine does not compete, or at least ought not to compete, with its offspring, for it appeals either to a different audience or to different tastes.

Roughly stated, the trouble is that the public for

these excellent magazines has changed, and they have not. Their public always was, and is, the so-called "refined" home public. Homes have changed, especially "refined" homes, and a new home means a new public.

The refined home nowadays has been to college. (There are a million college graduates now in the United States.) Forty years ago only scattered members had gone beyond the school. I do not propose to exaggerate the influence upon intelligence of a college education. It is possible, nay, it is common, to go through college and come out in any real sense uneducated. But it is not possible to pass through college, even as a professional amateur in athletics or as an inveterate flapper, without rubbing off the insulation here and there, without knowing what thought is stirring, what emotions are poignant, what ideas are dominant among the fraction of humanity that leads us. Refined homes may not be better or happier than they used to be, but if they are intellectual at all, they are more vigorously intellectual.

This means at the simplest that home readers of the kind I have been describing want stimulating food, not what our grandfathers used to call "slops." Sometimes they feed exclusively upon highly spiced journalism, but if they are literary in their tastes they will be less content with merely literary stories, with articles that are too solid to be good journalism, yet too popular to be profound, less content, in short, with dignity as a substitute for force.

What should be done about it specifically is a question for editors to answer. But this may be said. If the old literary omnibus is to continue, as it deserves, to hold the center of the roadway, then it must be driven with some vigor of the intellect to match the vigor of news which has carried its cheaper contemporary fast and far. By definition it cannot embrace a cause or a thesis, like the weeklies, and thank Heaven for that! It is clearly unsafe to stand upon mere dignity, respectability, or cost. That way lies decadence —such as overcame the old Quarterlies, the Annuals, and the periodical essayists. Vigor it must get, of a kind naturally belonging to its species, not violent, not raucous, not premature. It must recapture its public, and this is especially the "old American" (which does *not* mean the Anglo-Saxon) element in our mingled nation.

These old Americans are not moribund by any means, and it is ridiculous to suppose, as some recent importations in criticism do, that a merely respectable magazine will represent them. A good many of them, to be sure, regard magazines as table decorations, and for such a clientele some one some day will publish a monthly so ornamental that it will be unnecessary to read it in order to share its beneficent influences. The remainder are intellectualized, and many of them are emancipated from the conventions of the last generation, if not from those of their own. These demand a new vitality of brain, emotion, and spirit in their literary magazine, and it must be given to them.

No better proof of all this could be sought than the renaissance in our own times of the reviews and the weeklies, probably the most remarkable phenomenon in the history of American publishing since the birth of yellow journalism. By the weeklies I do not mean journals like *The Outlook, The Independent, Vanity Fair*, which are merely special varieties of the typically American magazine. I refer, of course, to *The New Republic, The Nation, The Freeman, The Weekly Review* in its original form, periodicals formed upon an old English model, devoted to the spreading of opinion, and consecrated to the propagation of intelligence. The success of these weeklies has been out of proportion to their circulation. Like the old *Nation*, which in a less specialized form was their predecessor, they have distinctly affected American thinking, and may yet affect our action in politics, education, and social relations generally. They are pioneers, with the faults of intellectual pioneers, over-seriousness, over-emphasis, dogmatism, and intolerance. Yet it may be said fairly that their chief duty, as with the editorial pages of newspapers, is to be consistently partisan. At least they have proved that the American will take thinking when he can get it. And by inference, one assumes that he will take strong feeling and vigorous truth in his literary magazines.

The reviews also show how the wind is blowing. The review, so-called, is a periodical presenting articles of some length, and usually critical in character, upon the political, social, and literary problems of the day. The distinction of the review is that its sober form and not too frequent appearance enable it to give matured opinion with space enough to develop it.

Clearly a successful review must depend upon a clientele with time and inclination to be seriously interested in discussion, and that is why the review, until recently, has best flourished in England where it was the organ of a governing class. In America, an intellectual class who felt themselves politically and socially responsible, has been harder to discover. We had one in the early days of the Republic, when *The North American Review* was founded. It is noteworthy that we are developing another now and have seen *The Yale Review*, the late lamented *Unpartisan Review*, and others join *The North American*, fringed, so to speak, by magazines of excerpt (of which much might be written), such as *The Review of Reviews, Current Opinion*, and *The Literary Digest*, in which the function of the review is discharged for the great community that insists upon reading hastily.

The review has come to its own with the war and reconstruction; which, considering its handicaps, is another argument that the family magazine should heed the sharpening of the American intellect. But, except for the strongest members of the family, it is still struggling, and still dependent for long life upon cheapness of production rather than breadth of appeal.

The difficulty is not so much with the readers as the writers. The review must largely depend upon the specialist writer (who alone has the equipment for specialist writing), and the American specialist cannot usually write well enough to command general intelligent attention. This is particularly noticeable in the minor reviews where contributions are not paid for and most of the writing is, in a sense, amateur, but it holds good in the magazines and the national reviews also. The specialist knows his politics, his biology, or his finance as well as his English or French contemporary, but he cannot digest his subject into words —he can think into it, but not out of it, and so cannot write acceptably for publication. Hence in science particularly, but also in biography, in literary criticism, and less often in history, we have to depend frequently upon English pens for our illumination.

The reasons for this very serious deficiency, much more serious from every point of view than the specialists realize, are well known to all but the specialists, and I do not propose to enter into them here. My point is that this very defect, which has made it so difficult to edit a valid and interesting review (and so creditable to succeed as we have in several instances succeeded), is a brake also upon the family magazine in its attempt to regain virility. The newspaper magazines have cornered the market for clever reporters who tap the reservoirs of special knowledge and then spray it acceptably upon the public. This is good as far as it goes, but does not go far. The scholars must serve us themselves—and are too often incapable.

Editorial embarrassments are increased, however, by the difficulty of finding these intellectualized old Americans who have drifted away from the old magazines and are being painfully collected in driblets by the weeklies and the reviews. They do not, unfortunately for circulation, all live in a London, or Paris. They are scattered in towns, cities, university communities, lonely plantations, all over a vast country. Probably that intellectualized public upon which all good magazines as well as all good reviews must depend, has not yet become so stratified and homogeneous after the upheavals of our generation that a commercial success of journalistic magnitude is possible, but it can and must be found.

The success of *The Atlantic Monthly* in finding a sizable and homogeneous public through the country is interesting in just this connection. It has, so it is generally understood, been very much a question of *finding*—of going West after the departing New Englander and his children, and hunting him out with the goods his soul desired. One remembers the Yankee peddlers who in the old days penetrated the frontier with the more material products of New England, pans, almanacs, and soap. But an observer must also note a change in the character of *The Atlantic* itself, how it has gradually changed from a literary and political review, to a literary and social magazine, with every element of the familiar American type except illustrations and a profusion of fiction; how in the attempt to become more interesting without becoming journalistic it has extended its operations to cover a wider and wider arc of human appeal. It has both lost and gained in the transformation, but it has undoubtedly proved itself adaptable and therefore alive. This is not an argument that the reviews should become magazines and that the old-line magazine should give up specializing in pictures and in fiction. Of course not. It is simply more proof that vigor, adaptability, and a keen sense of existing circumstances are the tonics they also need. The weekly lacks balance, the review, professional skill in the handling of serious subjects, the family magazine, a willingness to follow the best public taste wherever it leads.

It has been very difficult in this discussion, which I fear has resembled a shot-gun charge rather than a rifle bullet, to keep the single aim I have had in mind. The history of the periodical in American literary thinking has not yet been written. The history of American literature has but just been begun. My object has been to put the spotlight for a moment upon the typical American magazine, with just enough of its environment to make a background. What is seen there can best be summarized by a comparison. The American weekly is like the serious American play of the period. It has an over-emphasis upon lesson, bias, thesis, point. The review is like much American poetry. It is worthy, and occasionally admirable, but as a type it is weakened by amateur mediocrity in the art of writing. The family magazine is like the American short story. It has conventionalized into an often successful immobility. Both must move again, become flexible, vigorous, or their date will be upon them. And the family magazine, the illustrated literary magazine, is the most interesting vehicle of human expression and interpretation that we Americans have created. With a new and greater success, it will draw all our other efforts with it. If it fails, hope for the interesting review, the well-balanced weekly, is precarious. If they all submerge, we who like to read with discrimination and gusto will have to take to books as an exclusive diet, or make our choice between boredom and journalism.

III
The New Generation

The Young Romantics

WE have talked about the younger generation as if youth were a new phenomenon that had to be named and described, like a strange animal in the Garden of Eden. No wonder that our juniors have become self-conscious and have begun to defend themselves. Nevertheless, the generation born after the 'eighties has had an experience unique in our era. It has been urged, first by men and then by events, to discredit the statements of historians, the pictures of poets and novelists, and it has accepted the challenge. The result is a literature which speaks for the younger writers better, perhaps, than they speak for themselves, and this literature no reader whose brain is still flexible can afford to neglect; for to pass by youth for maturity is sooner or later to lose step with life.

In recent decades the novel especially, but also poetry, has drifted toward biography and autobiography. The older poets, who yesterday were the younger poets, such men as Masters, Robinson, Frost, Lindsay, have passed from lyric to biographic narrative; the younger poets more and more write of themselves. In the novel the trend is even more marked. An acute critic, Mr. Wilson Follett, has recently noted that the novel of class or social consciousness, which only ten years ago those who teach literature were discussing as the latest of late developments, has already given way to a vigorous rival. It has yielded room, if not given place, to the novel of the discontented person. The young men, and in a less degree the young women, especially in America, where the youngest generation is, I believe, more vigorous than elsewhere, have taken to biographical fiction. Furthermore, what began as biography, usually of a youth trying to discover how to plan his career, has drifted more and more toward autobiography—an autobiography of discontent.

There is, of course, nothing particularly new about biographical fiction. There is nothing generically new about the particular kind of demi-autobiographies that the advanced are writing just now. The last two decades have been rich in stories that need only a set of notes to reveal their approximate faithfulness to things that actually happened. But there is an emphasis upon revolt and disillusion and confusion in these latest novels that is new. They are no longer on the defensive, no longer stories of boys struggling to adapt themselves to a difficult world (men of forty-odd still write such stories); their authors are on the offensive, and with a reckless desire to accomplish their objectives, they shower us with such a profusion of detail, desert the paths of use and wont in fiction so freely, and so often disregard the comfort, not to speak of the niceties, of the reader, that "the young realists" has seemed a fair, although, as I think, a misleading title, for their authors. To a critic they are most interesting, for the novel of the alleged young realist is like a fresh country boy on a football field, powerful, promising, and utterly wasteful of its strength.

Recent American literature has been especially rich in such novels. There was, for example, Fitzgerald's ragged, but brilliant, "This Side of Paradise," which conducted aimless and expansive youth from childhood through college. There was the much more impressive "Main Street," biographic in form, but with teeth set on edge in revolt. There was the vivid and ill-controlled sex novel "Erik Dorn," and Evelyn Scott's "The Narrow House," in which the miseries of a young girl caught in the squalid and the commonplace had their airing. There was Stephen Benét's "The Beginning of Wisdom," where the revolt was a poet's, and the realist's detail selected from beauty instead of from ugliness; and Aikman's "Zell," in which youth rubs its sore shoulders against city blocks instead of university quadrangles. There was Dos Passos's "Three Soldiers," in which the boy hero is crushed by the war machine his elders have made. These are type examples, possibly not the best, certainly not the worst, drawn from the workshops of the so-called young realists.

What is the biography of this modern youth? His father, in the romantic 'nineties, usually conquered the life of his elders, seldom complained of it, never spurned it. His son-in-the-novel is born into a world of intense sensation, usually disagreeable. Instead of a "Peter Ibbetson" boyhood, he encounters disillusion after disillusion. At the age of seven or thereabout he sees through his parents and characterizes them in a phrase. At fourteen he sees through his education and begins to dodge it. At eighteen he sees through morality and steps over it. At twenty he loses respect for his home town, and at twenty-one discovers that our social and economic system is ridiculous. At twenty-three his story ends because the author has run through society to date and does not know what to do next. Life is ahead of the hero, and presumably a new society of his own making. This latter, however, does not appear in any of the books, and for good reasons.

In brief, this literature of the youngest generation is a literature of revolt, which is not surprising, but also a literature characterized by a minute and painful examination of environment. Youth, in the old days, when it rebelled, escaped to romantic climes or adventurous experience from a world which some one else had made for it. That is what the hacks of the movies and the grown-up children who write certain kinds of novels are still doing. But true youth is giving us this absorbed examination of all possible experiences that can come to a boy or girl who does not escape from every-day life, this unflattering picture of a world that does not fit, worked out with as much evidence as if each novel were to be part of a brief of youth against society. Indeed, the implied argument is often more important than the story, when there is a story. And the argument consists chiefly of *"this* happened to me," "I saw *this* and did not like it," "I was driven to *this* or *that,"* until the mass of circumstantial incident and sensation reminds one of the works of Zola and the scientific naturalists who half a century ago tried to put society as an organism into fiction and art.

No better example has been given us than Dos Passos's "Three Soldiers," a book that would be tiresome (and is tiresome to many) in its night after night and day after day crammed with every possible unpleasant sensation and experience that three young men could have had in the A. E. F. And that the experiences recorded were unpleasant ones, forced upon youth, not chosen by its will, is thoroughly characteristic. If it had not been for the rebellious pacifism in this book, it is questionable whether readers who had not been in France, and so could not relish the vivid reality of the descriptions, would have read to the end of the story.

The cause of all this is interesting, more interesting than some of the results. The full result we can scarcely judge yet, for despite signs of power and beauty and originality, only one or two of these books have reached artistic maturity; but we can prepare to comprehend it.

Here, roughly, is what I believe has happened, and if I confine my conclusions to fiction, it is not because I fail to realize that the effects are and will be far broader.

The youths of our epoch were born and grew up in a period of criticism and disintegration. They were children when the attack upon orthodox conceptions of society succeeded the attack upon orthodox conceptions of religion. We know how "the conflict between religion and science" reverberated in nineteenth-century literature and shaped its ends. The new attack was quite different. Instead of scrutinizing a set of beliefs, it scrutinized a method of living. Insensibly, the intelligent youth became aware that the distribution of wealth and the means of getting it were under attack; that questions were raised as to the rights of property and the causes and necessity of war. Soon moral concepts began to be shaken. He learned that prostitution might be regarded as an economic evil. He found that sex morality was regarded by some as a useful taboo; psychology taught him that repression could be as harmful as excess; the collapse of the Darwinian optimists, who believed that all curves were upward, left him with the inner conviction that everything, including principle, was in a state of flux. And his intellectual guides, first Shaw, and then, when Shaw became *vieux jeu*, De Gourmont, favored that conclusion.

Then came the war, which at a stroke destroyed his sense of security and with that his respect for the older generation that had guaranteed his world. Propaganda first enlightened him as to the evil meanings of imperialistic politics, and afterward left him suspicious of all politics. Cruelty and violent change became familiar. He had seen civilization disintegrate on the battlefield, and was prepared to find it shaky at home.

Then he resumed, or began, his reading and his writing. His reading of fiction and poetry, especially when it dealt with youth, irritated him. The pictures of life in Dickens, in "The Idylls of the King," in the Henty books, in the popular romantic novels and the conventional social studies, did not correspond with his pictures. They in no sense corresponded with the descriptions of society given by the new social thinkers whose ideas had leaked through to him. They did not square with his own experience. "The Charge of the Light Brigade" rang false to a member of the 26th Division. Quiet stories of idyllic youth in New England towns jarred upon the memories of a class-conscious youngster in modern New York. Youth began to scrutinize its own past, and then to write, with a passionate desire to tell the real truth, all of it, pleasant, unpleasant, or dirty, regardless of narrative relevance.

The result was this new naturalism, a propaganda of the experience of youth, where the fact that mother's face was ugly, not angelic, is supremely important, more important than the story, just because it was the truth. And as the surest way to get all the truth is to tell your own story, every potential novelist wrote his own story, enriching it, where sensation was thin, from the biographies of his intimates. Rousseau was reborn without his social philosophy. Defoe was reincarnated, but more anxious now to describe precisely what happened to him than to tell an effective tale.

This is a very different kind of truth-telling from, let us say, Mrs. Wharton's in "The Age of Innocence" or Zona Gale's in "Miss Lulu Bett." It does not spring from a desire to tell the truth about human nature.

These asserters of youth are not much interested in any human nature except their own, not much, indeed, in that, but only in the friction between their ego and the world. It is passionate truth, which is very different from cool truth; it is subjective, not objective; romantic, not classical, to use the old terms which few nowadays except Professor Babbitt's readers understand. Nor is it the truth that Wells, let us say, or, to use a greater name, Tolstoy was seeking. It is not didactic or even interpretative, but only the truth about the difference between the world as it is and the world as it was expected to be; an impressionistic truth; in fact, the truth about *my* experiences, which is very different from what I may sometime think to be the truth about mankind.

It will be strange if nothing very good comes from this impulse, for the purpose to "tell the world" that my vision of America is startlingly different from what I have read about America is identical with that break with the past which has again and again been prelude to a new era. I do not wish to discuss the alleged new era. Like the younger generation, it has been discussed too much and is becoming evidently self-conscious. But if the autobiographical novel is to be regarded as its literary herald (and they are all prophetic Declarations of Independence), then we may ask what has the new generation given us so far in the way of literary art.

Apparently the novel and the short story, as we have known them, are to be scrapped. Plot, which began to break down with the Russians, has crumbled into a maze of incident. You can no longer assume that the hero's encounter with a Gipsy in Chapter II is preparation for a tragedy in Chapter XXIX. In all probability the Gipsy will never be heard from again. She is irrelevant except as a figment in the author's memory, as an incident in autobiography. Setting, the old familiar background, put on the story like wall-paper on a living-room, has suffered a sea change also. It comes now by flashes, like a movie-film. What the ego remembers, that it describes, whether the drip of a faucet or the pimple on the face of a traffic policeman. As for character, there is usually but one, the hero; for the others live only as he sees them, and fade out when he looks away. If he is highly sexed, like Erik Dorn, the other figures appear in terms of sex, just as certain rays of light will bring out only one color in the objects they shine against.

The novel, in fact, has melted and run down into a diary, with sometimes no unity except the personality whose sensations are recorded. Many of us have wished to see the conventional story forms broken to bits. It was getting so that the first sentence of a short story or the first chapter of a novel gave the whole show away. We welcomed the English stories of a decade ago that began to give the complexities of life instead of the conventions of a plot. But this complete liquidation rather appals us.

The novels I have mentioned so far in this article have all together not enough plot to set up one lively

Victorian novel. Benét, Dos Passos, Fitzgerald—the flood-gates of each mind have been opened, and all that the years had dammed up bursts forth in a deluge of waters, carrying flotsam and jetsam and good things and mud.

It is not surprising that, having given up plot, these writers escape from other restraints also. The more energetic among them revel in expression, and it seems to make little difference whether it is the exquisite chiaroscuro of Chicago they are describing, or spots on a greasy apron. The less enthusiastic are content to be as full of gritty realistic facts as a fig of seeds; but with all of them everything from end to beginning, from bottom to top, must be said.

And just here lies the explanation of the whole matter. As one considers the excessive naturalism of the young realists and asks just why they find it necessary to be so excessively, so effusively realistic, the conviction is inborn that they are not realists at all as Hardy, Howells, even James were realists; they are romanticists of a deep, if not the deepest, dye, even the heartiest lover of sordid incident among them all.

I am aware, of course, that "romantic" is a dangerous word, more overworked than any other in the vocabulary of criticism, and very difficult to define. But in contrast with its opposites it can be made to mean something definite. Now, the romanticism of the juniors is not the opposite of realism; it sometimes embraces realism too lovingly for the reader's comfort. But it is the opposite of classicism. It is emotional expansiveness as contrasted with the classic doctrine of measure and restraint. By this, the older meaning of romanticism, we may put a tag upon the new men that will help to identify them. Their desire is to free their souls from the restraints of circumstance, to break through rule and convention, to let their hearts expand.

But they do not fly into Byronic melancholy or Wordsworthian enthusiasm for the mysterious abstract; they are far more likely to fly away from them. Byron and Wordsworth do not interest them, and Tennyson they hate. Romantic in mood, they are realistic, never classical, in their contact with experience. In poetry they prefer free verse, in prose they eschew grand phrases and sonorous words. It has been the hard realism of an unfriendly world that has scraped them to the raw, and they retaliate by vividly describing all the unpleasant things they remember. Taught by the social philosophers and war's disillusions that Denmark is decaying, they do not escape to Cathay or Bohemia, but stay at home and passionately narrate what Denmark has done to them. Romantic Zolas, they have stolen the weapons of realism to fight the battle of their ego. And the fact that a few pause in their naturalism to soar into idyllic description or the rapture of beauty merely proves my point, that they are fundamentally romantics seeking escape, and that autobiographical realism is merely romanticism *à la mode*.

Let us criticize it as such, remembering that we may be reading the first characteristic work of a new literary era. Let us give over being shocked. Those who were shocked by Byron, the apostle of expansiveness, merely encouraged him to be more shocking. Nor is it any use to sit upon the hydrant of this new expansiveness. If a youth desires to tell the world what has happened to him, he must be allowed to do so, provided he has skill and power enough to make us listen. And these juniors have power even when skill has not yet been granted them. What is needed is a hose to stop the waste of literary energy, to conserve and direct it. Call for a hose, then, as much as you please, but do not try to stop the waters with your Moses's rod of conservative indignation.

It is no crime to be a romantic,—it is a virtue, if that is the impulse of the age,—but it is a shame to be a wasteful romantic. Waste has always been the romantic vice—waste of emotion, waste of words, the waste that comes from easy profusion of sentiment and the formlessness that permits it. Think of "The Excursion," of Southey, and of the early poems of Shelley, of Scott at his wordiest. And these writers also are wasteful, in proportion to their strength.

They waste especially their imagination. Books like "The Three Soldiers" spill over in all directions—spill into poetry, philosophy, into endless conversation, and into everything describable. Books like "The Beginning of Wisdom" are still more wasteful. Here is the poignant biography of a boy who loves his environment even when it slays him, plus a collection of prose idylls,

plus a group of poems, plus a good piece of special reporting, plus an assortment of brilliant letters; and
imbedded in the mass, like a thread of gold in a tangle
of yarn, as fresh and exquisite a love-story as we have
had in recent English. Of course I do not mean that
all these elements cannot be woven into, made relevant
to, a theme, a story. Stendhal, himself a romantic, as
these men are romantics, could do it. But our romantics do not so weave them; they fling them out as
contributions to life's evidence, they fail to relate them
to a single interpretation of living, and half of the best
incidents are waste, and clog the slow-rolling wheels
of the story.

They waste their energy also. So keenly do they
love their own conception of true living that their imaginations dwell with a kind of horrid fascination upon
the ugly things that thwart them. Hence in a novel
like "Main Street," the interest slackens as one begins
to feel that the very vividness of the story comes from
a vision strained and aslant, unable to tear eyes from
the things that have cramped life instead of expanding
it. The things that these writers love in life often they
never reach until the last chapter, and about them
they have little to say, being exhausted by earlier
virulence.

Waste, of course, is a symptom of youth and vitality
as well as of unbridled romanticism, but that is no
reason for praising a book because it is disorderly.
We do not praise young, vigorous states for being disorderly. Life may not be orderly, but literature must

be. That is a platitude which it seems necessary to repeat.

It is difficult to estimate absolute achievement except across time, and the time has been too brief to judge of the merits of the young romanticists. My guess is that some of them will go far. But the diagnosis at present seems to show an inflammation of the ego. The new generation is discovering its soul by the pain of its bruises, as a baby is made aware of its body by pin-pricks and chafes. It is explaining its dissatisfactions with more violence than art.

Therefore at present the satirists and the educators hold the best cards, and most of them are elderly. No one of *les jeunes* writes with the skill, with the art, of Mrs. Wharton, Miss Sinclair, Tarkington, Galsworthy, or Wells. It should not long be so in a creative generation. In sheer emotion, in vivid protest that is not merely didactic, the advantage is all with the youngsters. But they waste it. They have learned to criticize their elders, but not themselves. They have boycotted the books of writers who were young just before themselves, but they have not learned to put a curb on their own expansiveness. We readers suffer. We do not appreciate their talents as we might, because we lose our bearings in hectic words or undigested incident. We lose by the slow realization of their art.

Youth is a disease that cures itself, though sometimes too late. The criticism I have made, in so far as it refers to youthful impetuosity, is merely the sort of thing that has to be said to every generation, and very loudly to the romantic ones. But if these auto-biographians are, as I believe, expansive romanticists, that is of deeper significance, and my hope is that the definition may prove useful to them as well as to readers who with an amazed affection persist in following them wherever they lead.

Puritans All

WHEN anything goes wrong in politics the American practice is to charge it against the Administration. In literature all grievances are attributed to the Puritans. If a well-written book does not sell, it is because the Puritans warped our sense of beauty; if an honest discussion of sex is attacked for indecency, it is the fault of the Puritan inheritance; if the heroes and heroines of new narratives in prose or verse jazz their way to destruction or impotence, it is in protest against the Puritans.

Who is this terrible Puritan? Apparently he is all America's ancestor, and whether you were born in Delaware or in South Carolina, in Montana or in Jugoslavia, you must adopt him as great-great-grandfather or declare yourself alien.

What was he, or rather, what did he stand for, and inflict upon us, to-day? Here there is some confusion. According to one set of critics he is not so much a hater of the arts as indifferent to their charms, not so much a Milton scornful of easy beauty, as a Philistine, deaf and blind to the esthetic. But these writers have apparently confounded Great-great-grandfather Puritan with Grandpa Victorian, the Victorian that Matthew Arnold scolded and Shaw made fun of. He is a type as different from the real Puritan as the slum dweller from the primitive barbarian. "Milton, thou shouldst be living at this hour" to flay such ignorant traducers of those who knew at least the beauty of austerity and holiness.

According to a less numerous but more clear-headed group of enemies the Puritan is to be censured chiefly for the rigidity of his conscience. He will not let us enjoy such "natural" pleasures as mirth, love, drinking, and idleness without a bitter antidote of remorse. He keeps books dull and reticent, makes plays virtuously didactic, and irritates all but the meek and the godly into revolt.

I am not an uncritical admirer of the Puritan, although I believe he is more nearly on the side of the angels than is his opposite. I deprecate the smug virtuosity which his kind often favor, I dislike a vinegar morality, and am repelled by the monstrous egoism of the idea that redeeming one's soul is such a serious matter that every moment spared from contemplating the sins of others or the pieties of oneself is irretrievably wasted.

But I object still more strongly to the anti-Puritans. Those rebels who make unconventionality their only convention, with their distrust of duty because they see no reason to be dutiful, and their philosophic nihilism, which comes to this, that all things having been proved false except their own desires, their desires become a philosophy, those anti-Puritans, as one sees them, especially in plays and on the stage, are an obstreperous, denying folk that seldom know their own minds to the end of the story. In fiction, distrusting what the Puritans call duty, they are left gasping in the last chapter, wondering usually what they are to do next; while the delightful lack of conscience that makes the flappers audacious and the young men so unremorsefully naughty leads to nothing at the end but a passionate desire to discover some new reason for living (which I take to mean, a new conscience) even if homes and social utility are wrecked in the attempt.

Why has duty become so unpopular in American literature? Is it because she is, after all, just what that loftiest if not most impeccable of Puritans called her, stern daughter of the voice of God? Is there to be no more sternness in our morals now we understand their psychology, no voice commanding us to do this or not to do that because there is a gulf set between worth and worthlessness? Is it true that because we are not to be damned for playing golf on Sunday, nothing can damn us? That because the rock-ribbed Vermont ancestor's idea of duty can never be ours, we have no duty to acknowledge? Is it true that if we cease being Puritans we can remain without principle, swayed only by impulse and events?

When these questions are answered to the hilt, we shall get something more vital than anti-Puritanism in modern American literature.

The Older Generation

THE American Academy of Arts and Letters says a word for the Older Generation now and then by choosing new academicians from its ranks. No one else for a long while now has been so poor as to do it reverence. Indeed, the readers of some of our magazines must have long since concluded that there are no fathers and mothers in the modern literary world, but only self-created heralds of the future who do not bother even to be rebellious against a generation they condemn.

The older generation is in a difficult situation, because, apparently, no one knows precisely who and what it is. The younger generation, of course, is made up of every one who dislikes Tennyson, believes in realism, reads De Gourmont, and was not responsible for the war. That is perfectly definite. We are somewhat puzzled by the uncounted hordes of the youthful in appearance who support the movies, are stolidly conservative in the colleges, never heard of De Gourmont, and have forgotten the war. But perhaps that is some other younger generation which no one has taken the trouble to write about—yet.

As for the older generation, what actually is it, and who in reality are they? The general impression seems to be that they are the Victorians, they are Howells and his contemporaries, they are the men and women who created the family magazine, invented morality, revived Puritanism, and tried to impose evolution on a society that preferred devolution by international combat. But these men are all dead, or have ceased writing. They are not *our* older generation. It is true that they are famous and so convenient for reference, but it is not accurate nor fair to drag them from their graves for purposes of argument.

The true older generation, of which one seldom hears in current criticism except in terms of abuse, remains to be discovered, and we herewith announce its personnel, so that the next time the youthful writer excoriates it in the abstract all may know just whom he means. Among the older generation in American literature are H. L. Mencken and Mrs. Edith Wharton, Booth Tarkington and Stuart P. Sherman, Miss Amy Lowell and Mr. Frank Moore Colby, Robert Frost and Edwin Arlington Robinson, Vachel Lindsay and Carl Sandburg, Mrs. Gerould and Professor William Lyon Phelps, Edgar Lee Masters, Joseph Hergesheimer, and most of the more radical editors of New York. Here is this group of desiccated Victorians, upholders of the ethics of Mr. Pickwick, and the artistic theories of Bulwer-Lytton. Here are the bogies of outworn conservatism, numbered like a football team. Mark their names, and know from now on that most of the books that you have supposed were solid in artistry and mature in thought, though perhaps novel in tone or in method, were written by the older generation.

Perhaps when the younger generation pretend to confuse their immediate predecessors with Ruskin and Carlyle, with Browning, Emerson, Hawthorne, Longfellow, and Matthew Arnold, they are merely strategic. For it is still dangerous to assault the citadels of the great Victorians with no greater books than the youthful volumes of 1918-1921, no matter how many breaches the war has left in the walls of their philosophy. It is far easier to assume that they are still alive in pallid survival, and to attack a hypothetic older generation, which, representing nothing real, can therefore not strike back.

Let the younger generation go back to its muttons, let it attend to its most pressing business, which is to create. It is vigorous, prolific, and, to my judgment, full of promise, but so far has done little or nothing not summarized in these words. It must pay its debt to time before it grows much older, or go down among expectations unrealized. It has few hours to waste upon attacking an older generation which, as it is described, does not exist except in youthful imagination, a generation actually of the middle-aged which in the meantime is bearing the burden of invention, creation, revolution in art while the youngsters are talking.

I should like to see less about the younger and more of this older generation in literary criticism. It is a fresh subject, scarcely touched by writers, and full of surprises. The jaded reader should be told that, in spite of rumors to the contrary, the middle-aged still exist.

A Literature of Protest

I HAVE pursued the discussions of the new American realism through university gatherings and literary inquests. Stripped of all metaphysics and relieved of all subtlety the conclusion of the matter is inescapable. It is not the realism of the realists, or the freedom of free verse, or the radicalism of the radical that in itself offends the critics, it is the growing ugliness of American literature. The harsh and often vulgar lines of Masters (so they say) seem to disdain beauty. Vachel Lindsay's shouted raptures are raucous. Miss Lowell's polyphonies have intellectual beauty, but the note is sharp, the splendors pyrotechnic. Robert Frost's restrained rhythms are homely in the single line. The "advanced" novelists, who win the prizes and stir up talk, are flat in style when not muddy in their English. They do not lift. An eighteenth century critic would call American literature ugly, or at least homely, if he dipped into its realities, rococo if he did not.

This is the sum of a criticism so strongly felt that it raises a barrier to appreciation, almost a gate shut against knowledge between the good American readers and the progressives in our literature. Sandburg and Lindsay between them will cause more acrimony in a gathering of English teachers than even Harold Bell

Wright. Miss Lowell carries controversy with her, triumphantly riding upon it. Their critics wish form as they have known form, want beauty such as they possess in riper literatures, want maturity, richness, suavity, grace, and the lift of noble thinking, nobly expressed. It may be remarked, in passing, that they also would like to live in English manors in gardened landscapes and have French cathedrals rise above their perfect towns!

It ought to be clear that we shall never get beauty of this kind, or of any absolute kind, in American writing until there is more beauty in American life. Amidst the vulgarities of signboards, cries of cheap newspapers, noisy hustle of trivial commercialism, and the flatness of standardized living, it is hard to feel spiritual qualities higher than optimism and reform. In general, wherever we have touched America we have made it uglier, as a necessary preliminary perhaps to making it anything at all, but uglier nevertheless. There was more hardship perhaps but also more clear beauty in Colonial days than in our own. More clear beauty, we say, because the present has its own vigorous beauty, more complex than what went before, but not yet clarified from the ugly elements that are making it. The forests and the skyscrapers are beautiful in America, but pretty much everything else below and between is soiled or broken by progress and prosperity.

And it is of the things in between, of America in the making, that these new writers, whose lack of pure beauty we deplore, and whose occasional gratuitous ugliness we dislike, are writing. They are protesting against its sordidness and crudity far more effectively than the cloistered reader who recites Shelley, saying "Why can't they write as he does." Like all that is human they share the qualities of their environment, like all fighters they acquire the faults of the enemy. They hate, often enough, the ugliness which a generation of progress has implanted in their own minds. They have been educated, perhaps, by the movies, Main Street conversation, formalized schools, and stale Methodism, and they hate their education. Or like the poets mentioned above they are moved by the pathos, the injustice, the confused beauty, the promise, not of some land of the past, but of the country under their feet, and write of what stirs them in terms that fit.

It is only when one understands this new American writing to be a literature of protest, that one begins to sympathize with its purposes, admire its achievements, and be tolerant of its limitations. For such a literature has very definite limitations. It is preparative rather than ultimate. The spaciousness of great imagination is seldom in it, and it lacks those grand and simple conceptions which generalize upon the human race. It is cluttered with descriptions of the enemy, it is nervous, or morbid, or excited, or over-emphatic. That it strikes out occasional sparks of vivid beauty, and has already produced masterpieces in poetry, is to be wondered at and praised.

But some one had to begin to write of the United States as it is. We could not go on with sentimental novels and spineless lyrics forever. Some writers had to refocus the instrument and look at reality again. And what the honest saw was not beautiful as Tennyson knew beauty, not grand, not even very pleasant. It is their job to make beauty out of it, beauty of a new kind probably, because it will accompany new truth; but they must have time. Surprise, shock, experiment, come first. The new literature deserves criticism, but it also deserves respect. Contempt for it is misplaced, aversion is dangerous since it leads to ignorance, wholesale condemnation such as one hears from professional platforms and reads in newspaper editorials is as futile as the undiscriminating praise of those who welcome novelty just because it is new.

Barbarians à la Mode

THE liberal mind, which just now is out of a job in politics, might very well have a look at the present state of literature. A task is there ready for it.

Our literature is being stretched and twisted or hacked and hewed by dogmatists. Most of the critics are too busy gossiping about plots and the private lives of authors to devote much attention to principles. But the noble few who still can write about a book without falling into it, or criticize an author's style without dragging in his taste in summer resorts, are chiefly concerned with classifications. Is our author conservative or radical? Are his novels long or short skirted? Does he write for *Harper's* or *The Dial?* They have divided America chronologically into the old and the new and geographically into East or West of the Alleghanies, or North or South of Fourteenth Street in New York. Such creative writers as have a definite philosophy of composition are equally categorical. And both are calling upon liberal minds, who are supposed to have no principles of their own, to umpire the controversy.

The liberal mind, which I believe in, though I hesitate to define it, has too much work before it to umpire in a dispute over the relative taste of the decayed and the raw. In literature, as in pretty much everything else, the central problem is not the struggle of the old

174

with the new; it is the endless combat of civilization (which is old *and* new) against barbarism. Under which banner our writers are enlisting is the vital question. Whether they are radical or conservative will always in the view of history be interesting, but may be substantially unimportant. And the function of the liberal mind, with its known power to dissolve illiberal dogmatism, is to discover the barbarian wherever he raises his head, and to convert or destroy him.

The Greeks had a short way of defining the barbarian which we can only envy. To them, all men not Greeks were barbarians. By this they meant that only the Greeks had learned to desire measure in all things, liberty safeguarded by law, and knowledge of the truth about life. Men not desiring these things were barbarous, no matter how noble, how rich, and how honest. The ancient and highly conservative Egyptians were barbarous; the youthful and new-fangled Gauls were barbarous. An Egyptian in nothing else resembled a Gaul, but both in the eyes of the Greek were barbarians.

Evolution and devolution have intervened. The Gaul has become one of the standards of civilization; the Egyptian has died of his conservatism; but the problem of the barbarian remains the same. There are neo-Gauls to-day and neo-Egyptians.

These gentry do not belong to the welter of vulgar barbarism, the curse of a half educated, half democratized age. They are found among the upper classes of the intellect, and can rightly be called by such names as conservative or radical, which show that they are part of the minority that thinks. Indeed, they are not barbarous at all in the harsh modern sense of the word; yet the Greeks would have condemned them.

The barbarism of the neo-Gaul is unrestraint ("punch" is the nearest modern equivalent). The neo-Gaul is an innovator and this is his vice. It is a by-product of originality and a symptom of a restless desire for change. The realist who makes a poem, not on his lady's eyebrows but her intestines, is a good current example. The novelist who shovels un-distinguished humanity, just because it is human, into his book is another. The versifier who twists and breaks his rhythm solely in order to get new sounds is a third. A fourth is the stylist who writes in disjointed phrases and expletives, intended to represent the actual processes of the mind.

The realist poet, so the Greeks would have said, lacks measure. He destroys the balance of his art by asking your attention for the strangeness of his subject. It is as if a sculptor should make a Venus of chewing gum. The novelist lacks self-restraint. Life interests him so much that he devours without digesting it. The result is like a moving picture run too fast. The versifier also lacks measure. He is more anxious to be new than to be true, and he seeks effects upon the reader rather than forms for his thought. The bizarre stylist misses truth by straining too much to achieve it. Words are only symbols. They never more than roughly represent a picture of thought. A monologue like this, as the heroine goes to shop:

Chapel Street . . . the old hardware shop . . . scissors, skates glittering, moonlight on the ice . . . old Dr. Brown's head, like a rink. Rink . . . a queer word! Pigeons in the air above the housetops—automobiles like elephants. Was her nose properly powdered? . . . Had she cared to dance with him after all?

is not absolutely true: it is not the wordless images that float through the idle mind, but only a symbol of them, more awkward and less informative than the plain English of what the heroine felt and thought.

All these instances are barbarous in the Greek sense, and their perpetrators, no matter how cultivated, how well-meaning, how useful sometimes as pioneers and pathbreakers, are barbarians. Some of them should be exposed; some chided; some labored with, according to the magnitude and the nature of their offense. The critics who uphold and approve them should be dealt with likewise. And it is the reader with the liberal mind who is called to the task. He is in sympathy, at least, with change, and knows that the history of civilization has been a struggle to break away from tradition and yet not go empty-handed; he can understand the passion to express old things in a new and better way, or he is not intellectually liberal. It takes a liberal mind to distinguish between barbarism and progress.

Next there is the *rigor mortis* of the neo-Egyptians, the barbarism of the dead hand, called by the unkind and the undiscriminating, academic barbarism.

Let us humor the Menckenites by so calling it, and

then add that it is by no means confined to the colleges, although it is a vice more familiar in critics than in creative artists. A Ph.D. is quite unnecessary in order to be academic in this sense, just as one does not have to be a scholar in order to be pedantical. To stand pat in one's thinking (and this is the neo-Egyptian fault) is to be barbarous, whatever the profession of the thinker. True, the victims of this hardening of the brain are precisely those men and women most likely to fling taunts at the moderns, just those who would rather be charged with immorality than barbarism. And yet, to be bound to the past is as barbarous in the Greek sense as to be wholly immersed in the present. The Egyptians for all their learning were barbarians.

Barbarian is not as rude a word as it sounds. Most of the great romanticists had strains of the barbarous in them—the young Shakespeare among them. Indeed, much may be said for sound barbarian literature, until it becomes self-conscious, though not much for barbarian criticism. Nevertheless, I do not intend in this sally against the slavish barbarism of the merely academic mind to hurl the epithet recklessly. Lusty conservatives who attack free verse, free fiction, ultra realism, "jazzed" prose, and the socialistic drama as the diseases of the period have my respect and sympathy, when it is a disease and not change as change that they are attacking. And, often enough, these manifestations *are* symptoms of disease, a plethoric disease arising from too high blood pressure. Hard-

hitting conservatives were never more needed in literature than now, when any one can print anything that
is novel, and find some one to approve of it. But there
are too many respectable barbarians among our American conservatives who write just what they wrote
twenty years ago, and like just what they liked twenty
years ago, because that is their nature. In 1600 they
would have done the same for 1579. Without question
men were regretting in 1600 the genius of the youthful
Shakespeare of the '80's, later quenched by commercialism (see the appeals to the pit and the topical
references in "Hamlet"); and good conservatives were
certainly regretting the sad course of the drama which,
torn from the scholars and flung to the mob, had become mad clowning. What we need in the Tory line
is not such ice-bound derelicts but men who are passionate about the past because they find their inspiration there, men and women who belabor the present
not for its existence, but because it might have been
better if it had been wiser.

They must, in short, be Greeks, not barbarians. It
is the reverse of barbarous to defend the old, but the
man who can see no need, no good, no hope in change
is a barbarian. He flinches from the truth physical
and the truth spiritual that life is motion. I particularly refer to the literary person who sneers at novels
because they are not epics, and condemns new poems
or plays unread if they deal with a phase of human
evolution that does not please him. I mean the critic
who drags his victim back to Aristotle or Matthew

Arnold and slays him on a text whose application
Aristotle or Arnold would have been the first to deny.
I mean the teacher who by ironic thrust and visible
contempt destroys the faith of youth in the literary
present without imparting more than a pallid interest
in the past. I mean the essayist who in 1911 described
Masefield as an unsound and dangerous radical in
verse, and in 1921 accepts him as the standard "modern" poet by whom his degenerate successors are to
be measured.

All this is barbarism because it is ignorance or denial
of the laws of growth. It belongs anthropologically
with totemism, sacerdotalism, neo-ritualism, and every
other remnant of the terrible shackles of use and wont
which chained early man to his past. It is Egyptian.
Its high priests are sometimes learned but their minds
are frozen. Beware of them.

In England, so far as I am able to judge, this variety
of barbarism shows itself usually in a rather snobbish
intolerance of anything not good form in literature.
The universities still protect it, but its home is in
London, among the professional middle class.

In America its symptom is well-disguised fear.
Some of us are afraid of our literary future just as
many of us are afraid of democracy. Poetry and criticism (we feel) which used to be written by classicists
and gentlemen are now in the hands of the corn-fed
multitude, educated God knows how or where. Fiction, once a profession, has become a trade, and so
has the drama. The line between journalism and litera-

ture is lost. Grub Street has become an emporium. Any one, anything can get into a story or a sonnet. . . .

The Greek of to-day (as we venture to define him) views all this with some regret, and more concern. He sees that fine traditions are withering, that fine things are being marred by ignorant handling. He fears debasement, he hates vulgarity, and his realist soul admits the high probability of both in a society whose standards are broader than they are high. But he also sees new energies let loose and new resources discovered; he recognizes new forms of expression, uncouth or colloquial perhaps, but capable of vitality and truth, and not without beauty. He bends his mind toward them, knowing that if he ignores them their authors will ignore him and his kind.

The Egyptian is afraid. He pulls his mantle closer about him and walks by on the other side.

Here again is work for the liberal mind. If it is really liberal—which means that training and disposition have made it free to move through both the past and the present—it can cope with this Egyptian barbarism; for liberal-minded lovers of literature, by performing a very simple operation in psychoanalysis, can understand how love for the good old times may cause fear lest we lose their fruits, and how fear blinds the critic's eye, makes his tongue harsh, and his judgment rigid as death.

Liberalism in politics is sulking just now, like Achilles in his tent, its aid having been invited too early, or too late. But the liberal spirit can never rest, and we solicit its help in literature. I have mentioned the Gauls and the Egyptians as the enemies within the camp of the intellectual, but beyond them lie the uncounted numbers of the outer barbarians, the mass of the unillumined, to whom neither tradition nor revolt, nor anything which moves and has its being in the intellect has any significance. Here is the common enemy of all, who can be conquered only by converting him. When the Gaul and the Egyptian are liberalized, the real job begins.

"If we compose well here, to Parthia."

IV

The Reviewing of Books

A Prospectus for Criticism

CRITICISM, in one respect, is like science: there is pure science, so-called, and applied science; there is pure criticism and applied criticism, which latter is reviewing. In applied science, principles established elsewhere are put to work; in reviewing, critical principles are, or should be, put to work in the analysis of books, but the books, if they are really important, often make it necessary to erect new critical principles. In fact, it is impossible to set a line where criticism ceases and reviewing begins. Good criticism is generally applicable to all literature; good reviewing is good criticism applied to a new book. I see no other valid distinction.

Reviewing in America has had a career by no means glorious. In the early nineteenth century, at the time of our first considerable productivity in literature, it was sporadic. The great guns—Lowell, Emerson— fired critical broadsides into the past; only occasionally (as in "A Fable for Critics") were they drawn into discussions of their contemporaries, and then, as in the Emerson-Whitman affair, they sometimes regretted it. Reviewing was carried on in small type, in the backs of certain magazines. Most of it was verbose and much of it was worthless as criticism. The belated recognition of the critical genius of Poe was due to the company he kept. He was a sadly erratic reviewer, as often wrong, I suppose, as right, but the most durable literary criticism of the age came from his pen, and is to be found in a review, a review of Hawthorne's short stories.

After the Civil War the situation did not immediately improve. We had perhaps better reviewing, certainly much better mediums of criticism, such, for example, as *The Nation,* and, later, *The Critic,* but not more really excellent criticism. The magazines and newspapers improved, the weekly, as a medium of reviewing, established itself, though it functioned imperfectly; the individuals of force and insight who broke through current comment into criticism were more plentiful, but not more eminent.

The new era in reviewing, our era, began with two phenomena, of which the first had obscure beginnings and the second can be exactly dated.

The first was modern journalism. Just when journalism became personal, racy, and inclusive of all the interests of modern life, I cannot say. Kipling exhibits its early effects upon literature, but Kipling was an effect, not a cause. No matter when it began, we have seen, in the decade or two behind us, reviewing made journalistic, an item of news, but still more a means of entertainment.

The journalistic reviewer, who is still the commonest variety, had one great merit. He was usually interesting. Naturally so, since he wrote not to criticize the book that had been given him, but to interest his readers. Yet by the very nature of the case he labored under a disadvantage which forever barred him from calling himself critic as well as reviewer. He was a specialist in reporting, in making a story from the most unpromising material, and also in the use of his mother tongue, but a specialist, usually, in no other field whatsoever. Fiction, poetry, biography, science, history, politics, theology—whatever came to his mill was grist for the paper, and the less he knew of the subject and the less he had read and thought, the more emphatic were his opinions.

The club and saber work of Pope's day and Christopher North's has gone—advertising has made it an expensive luxury, and here at least commercialism has been of service to literature. It was wholesale and emphatic praise that became a trademark of journalistic reviewing. First novels, or obscure novels, were sometimes handled roughly by a reviewer whose duty was to prepare a smart piece of copy. But when books by the well known came to his desk it was safer to praise than to damn, because in damning one had to give reasons, whereas indiscriminate praise needed neither knowledge nor excuse. Furthermore, since the chief object was to have one's review read, excessive praise had every advantage over measured approval. Who would hesitate between two articles, one headed "The Best Book of the Year," and the other, "A New Novel Critically Considered"!

Thus, journalism *per se* has done little for the cause

of American reviewing, and directly or indirectly it has done much harm, if only by encouraging publishers who found no competent discussions of their wares to set up their own critics, who poured out through the columns of an easy press commendations of the new books which were often most intelligent, but never unbiased.

The newspapers, however, have rendered one great service to criticism. In spite of their attempts to make even the most serious books newsy news, they, and they alone, have kept pace with the growing swarm of published books. The literary supplement, which proposed to review all books not strictly technical or transient, was a newspaper creation. And the literary supplement, which grew from the old book page, contained much reviewing which was in no bad sense journalistic. Without it the public would have had only the advertisements and the publishers' announcements to classify, analyze, and in some measure describe the regiment of books that marches in advance of our civilization.

We were not to be dependent, however, upon the budding supplements and the clever, ignorant reviewing, which, in spite of notable exceptions, characterized the newspaper view of books. The technical critic of technical books had long been practising, and his ability increased with the advance in scholarship that marked the end of the nineteenth century. The problem was how to make him write for the general intelligent reader. For years the old *Nation*, under the editorship of Garrison and of Godkin, carried on this struggle almost single-handed. For a generation it was the only American source from which an author might expect a competent review of a serious, non-technical book. But the weight of the endeavor was too much for it. Fiction it largely evaded, as the London *Times Literary Supplement* does to-day. And with all the serious books in English awaiting attention in a few pages of a single weekly, it is no wonder that the shelves of its editorial office held one of the best modern libraries in New York! Or that Christmas, 1887, was the time chosen to review a gift edition of 1886! The old *Dial* had a like struggle, and a resembling difficulty.

It was in 1914 that *The New Republic* applied a new solution to the problem, and from its pages and from the other "intellectual weeklies" which have joined it, has come not merely some of the best reviewing that we have had, but also a distinct lift upwards in the standard of our discussion of contemporary books of general interest. After 1914 one could expect to find American reviews of certain kinds of books which were as excellent as any criticisms from England or from France.

But the solution applied was of such a character as to limit definitely its application. *The New Republic,* the present *Nation, The Freeman, The Weekly Review,* and, in a little different sense, *The Dial,* were founded by groups held together, with the exception of *The Dial* coterie, not by any common attitude towards literature, or by any specific interest in literature itself, but rather by a common social philosophy. These journals, again with the one exception, were devoted primarily to the application of their respective social philosophies. Even when in reviews or articles there was no direct social application, there was a clear irradiation from within. When *The New Republic* is humorous, it is a social-liberal humor. When *The Freeman* is ironic there is usually an indirect reference to the Single Tax. And *The Dial* will be modern or perish.

As a result of all this the space given to books at large in the social-political journals was small. And in that space one could prophesy with some exactness the reviewing to be expected. Books of social philosophy, novels with a thesis, poetry of radical emotion, documented history, and the criticism of politics or economic theory have had such expert reviewing as America has never before provided in such quantity. But there was a certain monotony in the conclusions reached. "Advanced" books had "advanced" reviewers who approved of the author's ideas even if they did not like his book. Conservative books were sure to be attacked in one paragraph even if they were praised in another. What was much more deplorable, good, old-fashioned books, that were neither conservative nor radical, but just human, had an excellent chance of interesting no one of these philosophical editors and so of never being reviewed at all. Irving, Cooper of the Leatherstocking Series, possibly Hawthorne, and quite certainly the author of "Huckleberry Finn" would have turned over pages for many a day without seeing their names at all.

Thus the intellectual weekly gave us an upstanding, competent criticism of books with ideas in them— when the ideas seemed important to the editors; a useful service, but not a comprehensive one; the criticism of a trend rather than a literature; of the products of a social group rather than the outspeaking of a nation. Something more was needed.

Something more was needed; and specifically literary mediums that should be catholic in criticism, comprehensive in scope, sound, stimulating, and accurate.

To be catholic in criticism does not mean to be weak and opinionless. A determination to discuss literature honestly and with insight, letting conclusions be what they must, may be regarded as a sufficient editorial stock in trade. It is fundamental, but it is not sufficient. Just as there is personality behind every government, so there should be a definite set of personal convictions behind literary criticism, which is not a science, though science may aid it. Sterilized, dehumanized criticism is almost a contradiction in terms, except in those rare cases where the weighing of evidential facts is all that is required. But these cases are most rare. Even a study of the text of Beowulf, or a history of Norman law, will be influenced by the personal emotions of the investigator, and must be so criticized. Men choose their philosophy according to their temperament; so do writers write; and so must critics criticize. Which is by no means to say that criticism is merely an affair of temperament, but rather to assert that temperament must not be left out of account in conducting or interpreting criticism.

Ideally, then, the editors of a catholic review should have definite convictions, if flexible minds, established principles, if a wide latitude of application. But although a review may thus be made catholic, it cannot thus attain comprehensiveness. There are too many books; too many branches upon the luxuriant tree of modern knowledge. No editorial group, no editorial staff, can survey the field competently unless they strictly delimit it by selection, and that means not to be comprehensive. Yet if the experts are to be called in, the good critics, the good scholars, the good scientists, until every book is reviewed by the writer best qualified to review it, then we must hope to attain truth by averages as the scientists do, rather than by dogmatic edict. For if it is difficult to guarantee in a few that sympathy with all earnest books which does not preclude rigid honesty in the application of firmly held principles, it is more difficult with the many. And if it is hard to exclude bias, inaccuracy, over-statement, and inadequacy from the work even of a small and chosen group, it is still harder to be certain of complete competence if the net is thrown more widely.

In fact, there is no absolute insurance against bad criticism except the intelligence of the reader. He must discount where discount is necessary, he must weigh the authority of the reviewer, he must listen to the critic as the protestant to his minister, willing to be instructed, but aware of the fallibility of man.

Hence, a journal of comprehensive criticism must first select its reviewers with the greatest care and then print vouchers for their opinions, which will be the names of the reviewers. Hence it must open its columns to rebuttals or qualifications, so that the reader may form his own conclusions as to the validity of the criticism, and, after he has read the book, judge its critics.

All this is a world away from the anonymous, dogmatic reviewing of a century ago. But who shall say that in this respect our practice is retrograde?

It is a great and sprawling country, this America, with all manner of men of all manners in it, and the days of patent medicines have passed, when one bottle was supposed to contain a universal cure. But in this matter of reading, which must be the chief concern of those who support a critical journal, there is one disease common to most of us that can be diagnosed with certainty, and one sure, though slow-working, remedy, that can be applied. We are uncritical readers. We like too readily, which is an amiable fault; we dislike too readily, which is a misfortune. We accept the cheap when we might have the costly book. We dislike the new, the true, the accurate, and the beautiful, because we will not seek, or cannot grasp, them. We are afflicted with that complex of democracy—a distrust of the best. Nine out of ten magazines, nine out of ten libraries, nine out of ten intelligent American minds prove this accusation.

And the cure is more civilization, more intellectuality, a finer and stronger emotion? One might as well say that the cure for being sick is to get well! This, indeed, is the cure; but the remedy is a vigorous criticism. Call in the experts, let them name themselves and their qualifications like ancient champions, and then proceed to lay about with a will. Sometimes the maiden literature, queen of the tournament, will be slain instead of the Knight of Error, and often the spectators will be scratched by the whir of a sword. Nevertheless, the fight is in the open, we know the adversaries, and the final judgment, whether to salute a victor or condemn an impostor, is ours.

Thus, figuratively, one might describe the proper function in criticism of a liberal journal of catholic criticism to-day. One thing I have omitted, that its duty is not limited to criticism, for if it is to be comprehensive, it must present also vast quantities of accurate and indispensable facts, the news of literature. And one prerequisite I have felt it unnecessary to dwell upon. Unless its intent is honest, and its editors independent of influence from any self-interested source, the literary tournament of criticism becomes either a parade of the virtues with banners for the favorites, or a mêlée where rivals seek revenge. Venal criticism is the drug and dishonest criticism the poison of literature.

The Race of Reviewers

As a reviewer of books, my experience has been lengthy rather than considerable. It is, indeed, precisely twenty-two years since I wrote my first review, which ended, naturally, with the words "a good book to read of a winter evening before a roaring fire." I remember them because the publishers, who are lovers of platitudes, quoted them, to my deep gratification, and perhaps because I had seen them before. Since then I have reviewed at least twice as many books as there are years in this record—about as many, I suppose, as a book-page war-horse in racing trim could do in a month, or a week. My credentials are not impressive in this category, but perhaps they will suffice.

As an author, my claim to enter upon this self-contained symposium which I am about to present is somewhat stronger. Authors, of course, read all the reviews of their books, even that common American variety which runs like the telegraphic alphabet: quote—summarize—quote—quote—summarize—quote, and so on up to five dollars' worth, space rates. I have read all the reviews of my books except those which clipping bureaus seeking a subscription or kind friends wishing to chastise vicariously have neglected to send me. As an author I can speak with mingled feelings, but widely, of reviews.

Editorially my experience has been equally poignant. For ten years I have read reviews, revised and unrevised, in proof and out of it. I have cut reviews that needed cutting and meekly endured the curses of the reviewer. I have printed conscientiously reviews that had better been left unwritten, and held my head bloody but unbowed up to the buffets of the infuriated authors. As an editor I may say that I am at home, though not always happy, with reviewing and reviewers.

And now, when in one of those rare moments of meditation which even New York permits I ask myself why does every man or woman with the least stir of literature in them wish to review books, my trinitarian self—critic, author, editor—holds high debate. For a long time I have desired to fight it out, and find, if it can be found, the answer.

As an author, I have a strong distaste for reviewing. In the creative mood of composition, or in weary relaxation, reviewing seems the most ungrateful of tasks. Nothing comes whole to a reviewer. Half of every book must elude him, and the other half he must compress into snappy phrases. I watch him working upon that corpus, which so lately was a thing of life and movement—my book—and see that he cannot lift it; that he must have some hand-hold to grip it by— my style or my supposed interest in the Socialist Party, or the fact that I am a professor or a Roman Catholic. Unless he can get some phrase that will explain the characters of my women, the length of my sentences, and the moral I so carefully hid in the last chapter, he is helpless. Sometimes I find him running for a column without finding a gate to my mind, and then giving it up in mid-paragraph. Sometimes he gets inside, but dashes for the exit sign and is out before I know what he thinks. Sometimes he finds an idea to his liking, wraps up in it, and goes to sleep.

I recognize his usefulness. I take his hard raps meekly and even remember them when next I begin to write. I do not hate him much when he tells the public not to read me. There is always the chance that he is right for *his* public; not, thank heavens, for mine. I am furious only when it is clear that he has not read me himself. But I cannot envy him. It is so much more agreeable to make points than to find them. It is so much easier, if you have a little talent, to build some kind of an engine that will run than to explain what precise fault prevents it from being the best. When I am writing a book I cannot understand the mania for criticism that seems to infect the majority of the literary kind.

As a reviewer I must again confess, although as an editor I may bitterly regret the confession, that the passion for reviewing is almost inexplicable. Reviewing has the primal curse of hard labor upon it. You must do two kinds of work at once, and be adequately rewarded for neither. First you must digest another man's conception, assimilate his ideas, absorb his imagination. It is like eating a cold dinner on a full stomach. And then when you have eaten and digested, you must tell how you feel about it—briefly, cogently, and in words that cannot be misunderstood. Furthermore, your feelings must be typical, must represent what a thousand stomachs will feel, or should feel, or could feel if they felt at all, or instead of being hailed as a critic you will be accused of dyspepsia.

The mere mental labor of picking up the contents of a book as you proceed with your criticism, and tucking them in here and there where they fit, is so great that, speaking as a reviewer, I should give up reviewing if there were no more compelling reasons than requests to write criticism. There are, there must be; and still speaking as a reviewer I begin to glimpse one or two of them. Revenge is not one. Critics have written for revenge, quoting gleefully, "O that mine enemy would write a book!" Pope is our classic example. But publishers have made that form of literary vendetta unprofitable nowadays, and I am glad they have done so. Much wit, but little criticism, has been inspired by revenge. Furthermore, I notice in my own case, and my editorial self confirms the belief, that the reviewer craves books to extol, not books to condemn. He is happiest when his author is sympathetic to his own temperament. Antipathetic books must be forced upon him.

Which leads me to the further conclusion that the prime motive for reviewing is the creative instinct. We all of us have it, all of the literary folk who make up a most surprising proportion of every community in the United States. It works on us constantly. Sometimes it comes to a head and then we do a story

or a poem, an essay or a book; but in the meantime
it is constantly alive down below, drawn toward every
sympathetic manifestation without, craving self-expression and, in default of that, expression by others. If
a book is in us we write; if it is not, we seize upon
another man's child, adopt it as ours, talk of it, learn
to understand it, let it go reluctantly with our blessing,
and depart vicariously satisfied. That is the hope, the
ever-renewed hope, with which the besotted reviewer
takes up reviewing.

The creative instinct indeed is sexed, like the human
that possesses it. It seeks a mystical union with the
imaginings of others. The poet, the novelist, the essayist, seek the mind of the reader; the critic seeks the
mind of the writer. That we get so much bad reviewing is due to incompatibility of temperament or gross
discrepancy in the mating intellects. Yet reviewers
(and authors), like lovers, hope ever for the perfect
match.

I know one critic who tore his review in pieces because it revealed the charlatanism of his beloved author.
I know an author who burnt his manuscript because
his friend and critic had misunderstood him. I see
a thousand reviews (and have written several of them)
where book and reviewer muddle along together like the
partners of everyday marriages. But next time, one
always hopes, it will be different.

As an editor, I confess that I view all this effusion
with some distrust. One plain fact stands high and
dry above the discussion: books are being published

daily, and some one must tell the busy and none too discriminating public what they are worth—not to mention the librarians who are so engaged in making out triple cards and bibliographies and fitting titles to vague recollections that they have no time left to read. Furthermore, if reviewing is a chore at worst, and at best a desire to gratify a craving for the unappeasable, editing reviews is still more chorelike, and seeking the unobtainable—a good review for every good book—is quite as soul-exhausting as the creative instinct.

And, again as an editor, the perfect marriage of well attuned minds is well enough as an ideal, but as a practicable achievement I find myself more often drawn toward what I should call the liaison function of a reviewer. The desire to be useful (since we have excluded the desire to make money as a major motive) is, I believe, an impulse which very often moves the reviewer. The instinct to teach, to reform, to explain, to improve lies close to the heart of nine out of ten of us. It is commoner than the creative instinct. When it combines with it, one gets a potential reviewer.

The reviewer as a liaison officer is a homelier description than soul affinity or intellectual mate, but it is quite as honorable. Books (to the editor) represent, each one of them, so much experience, so much thought, so much imagination differently compounded in a story, poem, tractate on science, history, or play. Each is a man's most luminous self in words, ready for others. Who wants it? Who can make use of it? Who will be dulled by it? Who exalted? It is the reviewer's task to say. He grasps the book, estimates it, calculates its audience. Then he makes the liaison. He explains, he interprets, and in so doing necessarily criticizes, abstracts, appreciates. The service is inestimable, when properly rendered. It is essential for that growing literature of knowledge which science and the work of specialists in all fields have given us. Few readers can face alone and unaided a shelf of books on radio-activity, evolution, psychology, or sociology with any hope of selecting without guidance the best, or with any assurance that they dare reject as worthless what they do not understand. The house of the interpreter has become the literary journal, and its usefulness will increase.

A liaison of a different kind is quite as needful in works of sheer imagination. Here the content is human, the subject the heart, or life as one sees it. But reading, like writing, is a fine art that few master. Only the most sensitive, whose minds are as quick as their emotions are responsive, can go to the heart of a poem or a story. They need an interpreter, a tactful interpreter, who will give them the key and let them find their own chamber. Or who will wave them away from the door, or advise a brief sojourn. To an editor such an interpreter is an ideal reviewer. He will desire to be useful, and passionately attempt it. He will feel his responsibility first to art and next to the public, and then to his author, and last (as an editor I whisper it) to the publisher. Reviewers forget the author and the public. Their mandate comes from art (whose representative in the flesh is, or should be, the editor). But their highest service is to make a liaison between the reader and his book.

And the conclusion of this debate is, . I think, a simple one. Reviewing is a major sport, fascinating precisely because of its difficulty, compelling precisely because it appeals to strong instincts. For most of us it satisfies that desire to work for some end which we ourselves approve, regardless of costs. The editor, sardonically aware of a world that refuses to pay much for what men do to please themselves or to reform others, sees here his salvation, and is thankful.

The Sins of Reviewing

I HAVE known thousands of reviewers and liked most of them, except when they sneered at my friends or at me. Their profession, in which I have taken a humble share, has always seemed to me a useful, and sometimes a noble one; and their contribution to the civilizing of reading man, much greater than the credit they are given for it. We divide them invidiously into hack reviewers and critics, forgetting that a hack is just a reviewer overworked, and a critic a reviewer with leisure to perform real criticism. A good hack is more useful than a poor critic, and both belong to the same profession as surely as William Shakespeare and the author of a Broadway "show."

The trouble is that the business of reviewing has not been sufficiently recognized as a profession. Trades gain in power and recognition in proportion as their members sink individuality in the mass and form a union which stands as one man against the world. Professions are different. They rise by decentralization, and by specializing within the group. They gain distinction not only by the achievements of their individual members but by a curious splitting into subtypes of the species. Law and medicine are admirable examples. Every time they develop a new kind of specialist they gain in prestige and emolument.

A reviewer, however (unless he publishes a collected edition and becomes a critic), has so far remained in the eyes of the public just a reviewer. In fiction we have been told (by the reviewers) of romancers and realists, sociologists and ethicists, naturalists and symbolists, objectivists and psychologists. Are there no adjectives, no brevet titles of literary distinction for the men and women who have made it possible to talk intelligently about modern fiction without reading it?

My experience with reviewers has led me to classify them by temperament rather than by the theories they possess; and this is not so unscientific as it sounds, for theories usually spring from temperaments. No man whose eliminatory processes function perfectly is ever a pessimist, except under the compulsion of hard facts. No sluggish liver ever believes that joy of living is the prime quality to be sought in literary art. And by the same eternal principle, moody temperaments embrace one theory of criticism; cold, logical minds another. I identify my classes of reviewers by their habits, not their dogmas.

But in order to clear the ground let me make first a larger distinction, into mythical reviewers, bad but useful reviewers, bad and not useful reviewers, and good reviewers. Like the nineteenth century preacher I will dispose of the false, dwell upon the wicked, and end (briefly) with that heaven of literary criticism where all the authors are happy and all the reviewers excellent.

The reviewer I know best never, I profoundly believe, has existed, and I fear never will exist. He is the familiar figure of English novels—moderately young, a bachelor, with a just insufficient income in stocks. Oxford or Cambridge is his background, and his future is the death of a rich aunt or a handsome marriage. In the meantime, there is always a pile of books waiting in his chambers to be reviewed at "a guinea a page," when he has leisure, which is apparently only once or twice a week. The urban pastoral thus presented is one which Americans may well be envious of —*otium cum dignitate*. But I have never encountered this reviewer in London. I fear he exists only for the novelists, who created him in order to have a literary person with enough time on his hands to pursue the adventures required by the plot. Yet in so far as he is intended as a portrait of a critic, he stands as an ideal of the leisured view of books. There has been no leisured view of books in America since Thoreau, or Washington Irving. Even Poe was feverish. Our books are read on the subway, or after the theater, and so I fear it is in London—in London as it is.

Coldly, palpably real is the next critic of my acquaintance, the academic reviewer. He does not write for the newspapers, for he despises them, and they are rather scornful of his style, which is usually lumbering, and his idea that 1921 is the proper time in which to review the books of 1920. But you will find him in the weeklies, and rampant in the technical journals.

The academic reviewer is besotted by facts, or their

absence. The most precious part of the review to him is the last paragraph in which he points out misspellings, bad punctuation, and inaccuracies generally. Like a hound dog in a corn field, he never sees his books as a whole, but snouts and burrows along the trail he is following. If he knows the psychology of primitive man, primitive psychology he will find and criticize, even in a book on the making of gardens. If his specialty is French drama, French drama he will find, even in a footnote, and root it out and nuzzle it. I remember when a famous scholar devoted the whole of his review of a two volume *magnum opus* upon a great historical period, to the criticism of the text of a Latin hymn cited in a footnote! The academic reviewer (by which I do *not* mean the university reviewer, since many such are not academic in the bad sense which I am giving to the word) demands an index. His reviews usually end with, "There is no index," or, "There is an excellent index." The reason is plain. The index is his sole guide to reviewing. If he finds his pet topics there he can hunt them down remorselessly. But if there is no index, he is cast adrift helpless, knowing neither where to begin nor where to end his review. I call him a bad reviewer, but useful, because, though incapable of estimating philosophies or creations of the imagination, he is our best guarantee that writers' facts are facts.

My acquaintance with the next bad, but occasionally useful, reviewer is less extensive, but, by the circumstances of the case, more intimate. I shall call him the ego-frisky reviewer. The term (which I am quite aware is a barbarous compound) I am led to invent in order to describe the phenomenon of a critic whose ego frisks merrily over the corpus of his book. He is not so modern a product as he himself believes. The vituperative critics of the Quarterlies and, earlier still, of Grub Street, used their enemies' books as a means of indulging their needs for self-expression. But it was wrath, jealousy, vindictiveness, or political enmity which they discharged while seated on the body of the foe; whereas the ego-friskish critic has no such bile in him.

He is in fact a product of the new advertising psychology, which says, "Be human" (by which is meant "be personal") "first of all." He regards his book (I know this, because he has often told me so) as a text merely, for a discourse which must entertain the reader. And his idea of entertainment is to write about himself, his tastes, his moods, his reactions. Either he praises the book for what it does to his ego, or damns it for what it did to his ego. You will never catch him between these extremes, for moderation is not his vice.

The ego-frisky reviewer is not what the biologist would call a pure form. He (or she) is usually a yellow journalist, adopting criticism as a kind of protective coloration. The highly personal critic, adventuring, or even frolicking among masterpieces, and recording his experiences, is the true type, and it is he that the ego-friskish imitate. Such a critic in the jovial person of

Mr. Chesterton, or Professor Phelps, or Heywood Broun, contributes much to the vividness of our sense for books. But their imitators, although they sometimes enliven, more often devastate reviewing.

Alas, I am best acquainted among them all with the dull reviewer, who is neither good nor useful. The excellent books he has poisoned as though by opiates! The dull books he has made duller! No one has cause to love him unless it be the authors of weak books, who thank their dull critics for exposing them in reviews so tedious that no one discovers what the criticism is about.

The dull reviewer has two varieties: the stupid and the merely dull. It is the stupid reviewer who exasperates beyond patience the lover of good books. He is the man who gets a book wrong from the start, and then plods on after his own conception, which has no reference whatsoever to the author's. He is the man who takes irony seriously, misses the symbolism when there is any, and invariably guesses wrong as to the sources of the characters and the plot.

There are not many really stupid reviewers, for the most indolent editor cleans house occasionally, and the stupid are the first to go out the back door. But merely dull reviewers are as plentiful as fountain pens. The dull reviewer, like Chaucer's drunken man, knows where he wants to go but doesn't know how to get there. He (or she) has three favorite paths that lead nowhere, all equally devious.

The first is by interminable narrative. "When Hilda

was blown into the arms of Harold Garth at the windy corner of the Woolworth building, neither guessed at what was to follow. Beginning with this amusing situation, the author of 'The Yellow Moon' develops a very interesting plot. Garth was the nephew of Miles Harrison, Mayor of New York. After graduating from Williams, etc., etc., etc." This is what he calls summarizing the plot.

Unfortunately, the art of summary is seldom mastered, and a bad summary is the dullest thing in the world. Yet even a bad summary of a novel or a book of essays is hard to do; so that when the dull reviewer has finished, his sweaty brow and numbed fingers persuade him that he has written a review. There is time for just a word of quasi-criticism: "This book would have been better if it had been shorter, and the plot is not always logical. Nevertheless, 'The Yellow Moon' holds interest throughout." And then, finis. This is botchery and sometimes butchery, not reviewing.

The dullest reviewers I have known, however, have been the long-winded ones. A book is talk about life, and therefore talk about a book is one remove more from the reality of experience. Talk about talk must be good talk, and it must be sparing of words. A concise style is nearly always an interesting style: even though it repel by crudity it will never be dull. But conciseness is not the quality I most often detect in reviewing. It is luxurious to be concise when one is writing at space rates; and it is always harder to say a thing briefly than at length, just as it is easier for a woman to hit a nail at the third stroke than at the first.

I once proposed a competition in a college class in English composition. Each student was to clip a col- umn newspaper article of comment (not facts) and condense it to the limit of safety. Then editorials gave up their gaseous matter in clouds, chatty news stories boiled away to paragraphs, and articles shrank up to their headlines.

But the reviews suffered most. One, I remember, came down to "It is a bad book," or to express it algebraically, (It is a bad book)^3. Another disappeared entirely. On strict analysis it was discovered that the reviewer had said nothing not canceled out by some- thing else. But most remained as a weak liquor of comment upon which floated a hard cake of undigested narrative. One student found a bit of closely reasoned criticism that argued from definite evidences to a con- crete conclusion. It was irreducible; but this was a unique experience.

The long-winded are the dullest of dull reviewers, but the most pernicious are the wielders of clichés and platitudes. Is there somewhere a reviewer's manual, like the manual of correct social phrases which some one has recently published? I would believe it from the evidence of a hundred reviews in which the same phrases, differently arranged, are applied to fifty dif- ferent books. I would believe it, except for the known capacity of man to borrow most of his thoughts and all of his phrases from his neighbor. I know too well that writers may operate like the Federal Reserve banks, except that in literature there is no limit to inflation. A thousand thousand may use "a novel of daring adventure," "a poem full of grace and beauty," or "shows the reaction of a thoughtful mind to the facts of the universe," without exhausting the supply. It is like the manufacture of paper money, and the effect on credit is precisely the same.

So much for the various types of reviewers who, however interesting they may be critically, cannot be called good. The good reviewers, let an uncharitable world say what it will, are, thank heaven! more numerous. Their divisions, temperamental and intellectual, present a curious picture of the difficulties and the rewards of this profession. Yet I cannot enter upon them here, and for good reasons.

The good reviewer is like the good teacher and the good preacher. He is not rare, but he is precious. He has qualities that almost escape analysis and therefore deserve more than a complimentary discussion. He must hold his book like a crystal ball in which he sees not only its proper essence in perfect clarity, but also his own mind mirrored. He must— . . . In other words, the good reviewer deserves an essay of his own. He is a genius in a minor art, which sometimes becomes major; a craftsman whose skill is often exceptional. I will not put him in the same apartment with reviewers who are arid, egoistic, or dull.

Mrs. Wharton's "The Age of Innocence"

AMERICA is the land of cherished illusions. Americans prefer to believe that they are innocent, innocent of immorality after marriage, innocent of dishonesty in business, innocent of incompatibility between husbands and wives. Americans do not like to admit the existence (in the family) of passion, of unscrupulousness, of temperament. They have made a code for what is to be done, and what is not to be done, and whatever differs is un-American. If their right hands offend them they cut them off rather than admit possession. They believed in international morality when none existed, and when they were made to face the disagreeable fact of war, cast off the nations of the earth, and continued to believe in national morality.

In America prostitution is tolerated in practice, but forbidden in print. All homes are happy unless there is proof to the contrary, and then they are un-American. In its wilful idealism America is determined that at all costs we shall appear to be innocent. And a novel which should begin with the leaders in social conformity, who keep hard and clean the code, and should sweep through the great middle classes that may escape its rigors themselves, but exact them of others, might present the pageant, the social history, the epic of America.

Of course, Mrs. Wharton's novel does nothing of the sort. This is how Tolstoy, or H. G. Wells, or Ernest Poole would have written "The Age of Innocence." They would have been grandiose, epical; their stories would have been histories of culture. It would have been as easy to have called their books broad as it is to call Mrs. Wharton's fine novel narrow. Tendencies, philosophies, irrepressible outbursts would have served as their protagonists, where hers are dwellers in Fifth Avenue or Waverly Place—a cosmopolitan astray, a dowager, a clubman yearning for intellectual sympathy.

And yet in the long run it comes to much the same thing. The epic novelists prefer the panorama: she the drawing-room canvas. They deduce from vast philosophies and depict society. She gives us the Mingotts, the Mansons, the Van der Luydens—society, in its little brownstone New York of the '70's—and lets us formulate inductively the code of America. A little canvas is enough for a great picture if the painting is good.

Indeed, the only objection I have ever heard urged against Mrs. Wharton's fine art of narrative is that it is narrow—an art of dress suit and sophistication. And this book is the answer. For, of course, her art is narrow—like Jane Austen's, like Sheridan's, like Pope's, like Maupassant's, like that of all writers who prefer to study human nature in its most articulate instead of its broadest manifestations. It is narrow because it is focussed, but this does not mean that it

is small. Although the story of "The Age of Innocence" might have been set in a far broader background, it is the circumstances of the New York society
which Mrs. Wharton knows so well that give it a
piquancy, a reality that "epics" lack. They are like
the accidents of voice, eye, gesture which determine
individuality. Yet her subject is America.

This treating of large themes by highly personal symbols makes possible Mrs. Wharton's admirable perfection of technique. Hers is the technique of sculpture
rather than the technique of architecture. It permits
the fine play of a humor that has an eye of irony in
it, but is more human than irony. It makes possible
an approach to perfection. Behold Mrs. Manson Min-
gott, the indomitable dowager, Catherine:

> The immense accretions of flesh which had descended on
> her in middle life, like a flood of lava on a doomed city had
> changed her . . . into something as vast and august as a
> natural phenomenon. She had accepted this submergence as
> philosophically as all her other trials, and now, in extreme
> old age, was rewarded by presenting to her mirror an almost
> unwrinkled expanse of firm pink and white flesh, in the
> center of which the traces of a small face survived as if
> awaiting excavation. . . . Around and below, wave after
> wave of black silk surged away over the edges of a capacious
> armchair, with two tiny white hands poised like gulls on the
> surface of the billows.

Her art is restrained, focussed upon those points
where America, in its normality and in its eccentricity,

has become articulate. Therefore it is sharp and convincing.

Who is the central figure in this story where the leaven of intellectual and emotional unrest works in a society that has perfected its code and intends to live by it? Is it Newland Archer, who bears the uncomfortable ferment within him? Is it his wife, the lovely May, whose clear blue eyes will see only innocence? Is it the Countess Olenska, the American who has seen reality and suffered by it, and sacrifices her love for Newland in order to preserve his innocence? No one of these is the center of the story, but rather the idea of "the family," this American "family," which is moral according to its lights, provincial, narrow—but intensely determined that its world shall appear upright, faithful, courageous, in despite of facts, and regardless of how poor reality must be tortured until it conforms. And the "family" as Mrs. Wharton describes it is just the bourgeois Puritanism of nineteenth century America.

Was May right when, with the might of innocence, she forced Newland to give up life for mere living? Was the Countess right when, in spite of her love for him, she aided and abetted her, making him live up to the self-restraint that belonged to his code? The story does not answer, being concerned with the qualities of the "family," not with didacticism.

It says that the insistent innocence of America had its rewards as well as its penalties. It says, in so far as it states any conclusion definitely, that a new and less trammeled generation must answer whether it was the discipline of its parents that saved the American family from anarchy, or the suppressions of its parents that made it rebellious. And the answer is not yet.

"The Age of Innocence" is a fine novel, beautifully written, "big" in the best sense, which has nothing to do with size, a credit to American literature—for if its author is cosmopolitan, this novel, as much as her earlier "Ethan Frome," is a fruit of our soil.

November 6, 1920.

Mr. Hergesheimer's "Cytherea"

MRS. WHARTON found the age of innocence in the
1870's; Mr. Hergesheimer discovers an age of no innocence in the 1920's. In "The Age of Innocence," the
lovely May, a creature of society's conventions, loses
her husband and then regains the dulled personality
left from the fire of passion. In "Cytherea" the less
lovely, but equally moral Fanny loses her Lee because
she cannot satisfy his longings and nags when she fails.
But she does not regain him when his love chase is
over, because he is burned out. Athene and Aphrodite,
the graces of the mind, the seductions of the person
of the Countess Olenska, together draw Newland
Archer, husband of May; but it is Aphrodite only,
Cytherean Aphrodite, who, being sex incarnate, is more
than mere temptations of the flesh, that wrecks Fanny's
home.

In the '70's the poor innocents of society believed
their code of honor impregnable against sex. They
dressed against sex, talked against sex, kept sex below
the surface. The suppression froze some of them into
rigidity and stiffened all. But they had their compensations. By sacrificing freedom for personal desire
they gained much security. Good husbands required
more than a lure of the body to take them off. And
when they gave up a great romance for respectability,

like Newland Archer, at least they remained gentlemen.
There was a tragedy of thwarted development, of mar-
tyred love, of waste; but at least self-respect, however
misguided, remained.

Not so with this trivial, lawless country club set of
the 1920's, drunk part of the time and reckless all of
it, codeless, dutiless, restless. For the virtuous among
them Aphrodite, a vulgar, shameless Aphrodite, was a
nightly menace; for the weak among them (such as
Peyton Morris), a passion to be resisted only by fear;
for the wayward, like Lee, she was the only illusion
worth pursuing. To resist for a woman was to become
"blasted and twisted out of her purpose," to be
"steeped in vinegar or filled with tallow"; to resist for
a man was to lose the integrity of his personality.
There were no moral compensations, for there is no
morality but self-development, at least in Mr. Hergesheimer's town of Eastlake. There is no god for a man
in love but Cytherea.

And this is one way of describing Mr. Hergesheimer's
study of love in idleness in the 1920's. Another way
would be to call it an essay upon insecurity, although
the word essay is too dry to use in a story which is fairly
awash with alcohol. The war, the story seems to say,
sapped our security of property and comfort and life.
But insecurity is an insidious disease that spreads, like
bacteria, where strength is relaxed. It infects the lives
of those who have lost their certainties and become
doubtful of their wills. In this relaxed society of the
1920's, where nothing seemed certain but the need of

money and a drink, insecurity spread into married life. Not even the well-mated were secure in the general decline of use and wont. A home wrecked by vague desires running wild—that is the theme of "Cytherea."

Or take a third view of this provocative book. The triangle we have had tiresomely with us, but it is woman's love that is, perversely, always the hero. Hergesheimer studies the man, studies him not as will, or energy, or desire a-struggle with duty or morality, but merely as sex. Man's sex in love, man's sex dominated by Cytherea, is his theme. This is new, at least in fiction, for there man is often swept away, but seldom dominated by sex. And indeed Hergesheimer has to find his man in the relaxed society to which I have referred, a society wearied by unchartered freedom, where business is profitable but trivial, where duty and religion exist only as a convention, disregarded by the honest, upheld by the hypocritical, a society where Cytherea marks and grips her own. Even so, it is an achievement.

Cytherea in the story is a doll with a glamorous countenance, bought and cherished by Lee Randon as a symbol of what he did not find in his married life, what no man finds and keeps, because it is an illusion. Cytherea is Lee Randon's longing for emotional satisfaction, a satisfaction that is not to be of the body merely. And when he meets Savina Grove, a pathological case, whose violent sex emotions have been inhibited to the bursting point, he thinks (and fears) that he has found his heart's desire. In the old, old stories their elopement would have been their grand, their tragic romance. In this cruel novel it is tragic, for she dies of it; but she is not Cytherea; she is earthly merely; it is felt that she is better dead.

It is a cruel story, cruel in its depiction of an almost worthless society with just enough of the charm of the Restoration to save it from beastliness; cruel in its unsparing analyses of man's sex impulses (by all odds the most valuable part of the story); cruel particularly because the ruined Lee Randon is a good fellow, honester than most, kinder than he knows to individuals, although certain that there is no principle but selfishness, and that it is folly to limit desire for the sake of absolutes, like righteousness, or generalities, like the human race. It is a cruel study of women, for Fanny, the model of the domestic virtues, has lost her innocent certainties of the triumph of the right and at the first conflict with Cytherea becomes a common scold; cruel to Savina Grove, who, in spite of her exquisiteness, is only a psychoanalyst's problem; cruel to us all in exposing so ruthlessly how distressing it is to live by stale morality, yet how devastating to act with no guide but illusory desire.

All this is not new in outline. One can find the essence of this story in monkish manuals. There the menace of Cytherea was not evaded. There the weaknesses of man's sex were categoried with less psychology but more force. What is new in Hergesheimer's book is merely the environment in which his characters so disastrously move and an insight into the mechanism of their psychology which earlier writers lacked. I have called it a story of the age of no innocence, but that would be the author's term, not mine; for indeed his characters seem to display as naïve an innocence as Mrs. Wharton's of the laws of blood and will, and they know far less of practical morality. The "Age of Moral Innocence" I should rechristen Hergesheimer's book.

Critics will raise, and properly, a question as to the worth of his materials. He is not studying a "ripe" society, as was Mrs. Wharton, but the froth of the war, the spume of country clubs, the trivialities of the strenuous but unproductive rich. This is a just criticism as far as it goes, and it lessens the solidity, the enduring interest, of his.achievement. True, it was in such a society that he could best pursue the wiles of Cytherea. He has a right to pitch his laboratory where he pleases, and out of some very sordid earth he has contrived some beauty. Nevertheless, you cannot make a silk purse out of a sow's ear, skilled though you may be.

I should be more inclined, however, in a comparison with Mrs. Wharton, to criticize his lack of detachment. That able novelist, who is bounded so exclusively in her little social world, nevertheless stands apart from it and sees it whole. Mr. Hergesheimer has his feet still deep in the soil. He is too much a part of his country club life. He means, perhaps, to be ironical, but in truth he is too sympathetic with the desires, emotional and esthetic, that he expresses to be ironical until the close. There is a surprise, too sharp a surprise, at the end of his novel, when one discovers that the moral is not "do and dare," but "all is vanity." He is so much and so lusciously at home with cocktails, legs, limousine parties, stair-sittings, intra-matrimonial kissings (I mention the most frequent references) that one distrusts the sudden sarcasm of his finale. It would have been better almost if he had been a Count de Gramont throughout, for he has a *flair* for the surroundings of amorous adventure and is seldom gross; better still to have seen, as Mrs. Wharton saw, the picture in perspective from the first. His book will disgust some and annoy others because its art is muddied by a lingering naturalism and too highly colored by the predilections of the artist.

It is a skilful art, nevertheless, and "Cytherea" confirms a judgment long held that Mr. Hergesheimer is one of the most skilful craftsmen in English in our day. And this I say in spite of his obvious failure to grasp inevitably the structure of the English sentence. He is one of the most honest analysts of a situation, also; one of the most fearless seekers of motives; one of the ablest practisers of that transmutation of obscure emotion into the visible detail of dress, habit, expression, which is the real technique of the novelist. His fault is a defect in sympathy, a lack of spiritual appreciation, if I may use and leave undefined so old-fashioned a term. His virtue lies in the rich garment of experience which careful observation and skilful writing enable him to wrap about his imaginative conceptions. It is this which makes his novels so readable for the discriminating at present, and will make them useful historical records in the future. One aspect of a troublesome period when the middle generation achieved the irresponsibility without the earnestness of youth he has caught in "Cytherea." It is unfortunate that it is a partial portrait of important motives in people who themselves are of little importance; and it is doubly unfortunate that he has been too much a part of his muddy world to be as good an interpreter as he is a witness of its life.

January 21, 1922.

V
Philistines and Dilettante

Poetry for the Unpoetical

I HAVE looked through more essays upon poetry than I care to remember without finding anywhere a discussion of poetry for the unpoetical. A recent writer, it is true, has done much to show that the general reader daily indulges in poetry of a kind without knowing it. But the voluminous literature of poetics is well-nigh all special. It is written for students of rhythm, for instinctive lovers of poetry, for writers of verse, for critics. It does not treat of the value of poetry for the average, the unpoetical man—it says little of his curious distaste for all that is not prose, or of the share in all good poetry that belongs to him.

By the average man, let me hasten to say, I mean in this instance the average intelligent reader, who has passed through the usual formal education in literature, who reads books as well as newspapers and magazines, who, without calling himself a littérateur, would be willing to assert that he was fairly well read and reasonably fond of good reading. Your doctor, your lawyer, the president of your bank, and any educated business man who has not turned his brain into a machine, will fit my case.

Among such excellent Americans, I find that there exists a double standard as regards all literature, but

especially poetry. Just as the newspapers always write
of clean politics with reverence—whatever may be the
private opinions and practices of their editorial writers
—so intelligent, though unpoetic, readers are accustomed to speak of poetry with very considerable respect. It is not proper to say, "I hate poetry," even
if one thinks it. To admit ignorance of Tennyson or
Milton or Shakespeare is bad form, even if one skimmed
through them in college and has never disturbed the
dust upon their covers since. I have heard a whispered,
sneering remark after dinner, "I don't believe he ever
heard of Browning," by one who had penetrated about
as far into Browning's inner consciousness as a fly
into the hickory-nut it crawls over. I well remember
seeing a lady of highly respectable culture hold up her
hands in horror before a college graduate who did not
know who Beowulf was. Neither did she, in any true
sense of knowing. But her code taught her that the
"Beowulf," like other "good poetry," should be upon
one's list of acquaintances.

What these Americans really think is a very different
matter. The man in the trolley-car, the woman in the
rocking-chair, the clerk, the doctor, the manufacturer,
most lawyers, and some ministers would, if their hearts
were opened, give simply a categorical negative. They
do not like poetry, or they think they do not like it;
in either case with the same result. The rhythm an-
noys them (little wonder, since they usually read it
as prose), the rhyme seems needless, the inversions,
the compressions perplex their minds to no valuable

end. Speaking honestly, they do not like poetry. And if their reason is the old one,

> I do not like you, Dr. Fell;
> The reason why I cannot tell,

it is none the less effective.

But the positive answers are no more reassuring. Here in America especially, when we like poetry, we like it none too good. The "old favorites" are almost all platitudinous in thought and monotonous in rhythm. We prefer sentiment, and have a weakness for slush. Pathos seems to us better than tragedy, anecdote than wit. Longfellow was and is, except in metropolitan centres, our favorite "classical" poet; the poetical corner and the daily poem of the newspapers represent what most of us like when we do go in for verse. The truth is that many of the intelligent in our population skip poetry in their reading just because it *is* poetry. They read no poetry, or they read bad poetry occasionally, or they read good poetry badly.

This sorry state of affairs does not trouble the literary critic. His usual comment is that either one loves poetry or one does not, and that is all there is to be said about it. If the general reader neglects poetry, why then he belongs to the Lost Tribes and signifies nothing for Israel.

I am sure that he is wrong. His assertion is based on the theory that every man worthy of literary salvation must at all times love and desire the best literature, which is poetry—and this is a fallacy. It is as absurd as if he should ask most of us to dwell in religious exaltation incessantly, or to live exclusively upon mountain peaks, or to cultivate rapture during sixteen hours of the twenty-four. The saints, the martyrs, the seers, the seekers, and enthusiasts have profited nobly by such a régime, but not we of common clay. To assume in advocating the reading of poetry that one should substitute Pope for the daily paper, Francis Thompson for the illustrated weekly, *The Ring and the Book* for a magazine, and read "The Golden Treasury" through instead of a novel, needs only to be stated to be disproved. And yet this is the implication of much literary criticism.

But the sin of the general reader who refuses all poetry is much more deadly, for it is due not to enthusiasm, but to ignorance. It is true that the literary diet recommended by an esthetic critic would choke a healthy business man; but it is equally true that for all men whose emotions are still alive within them, and whose intelligence permits the reading of verse, poetry is quite as valuable as fresh air and exercise. We do not need fresh air and exercise constantly. We can get along very comfortably without them. But if they are not essential commodities, they are important ones, and so is poetry—a truth of which modern readers seem to be as ignorant as was primitive man of fire until he burned his hand in a blazing bush.

I do not mean for an instant to propose that every one should read poetry. The man whose imagination has never taken fire from literature of any kind, whose brain is literal and dislikes any embroidery upon the surface of plain fact, who is deaf to music, unresponsive to ideas, and limited in his emotions—such a man in my opinion is unfortunate, although he is often an excellent citizen, lives happily, makes a good husband, and may save the state. But he should not (no danger that he will) read poetry. And for another class there is nothing in poetry. The emotionally dying or dead; the men who have sunk themselves, their personalities, their hopes, their happiness, in business or scholarship or politics or sport—they, too, are often useful citizens, and usually highly prosperous; but they would waste their time upon literature of any variety, and especially upon poetry.

There are a dozen good arguments, however, to prove that the reading of poetry is good for the right kind of general reader, who is neither defective nor dead in his emotions; and this means, after all, a very large percentage of all readers. If I had space I should use them all, for I realize that the convention we have adopted for poetry makes us skip, in our magazines, as naturally from story to story over the verse between as from stone to stone across the brook. However, I choose only two, which seem to me as convincing for the unpoetical reader (the dead and defective excepted) as the ethical grandeur of poetry, let us say, for the moralist, its beauty for the esthete, its packed knowledge for the scholar.

The first has often been urged before and far more often overlooked. We everyday folk plod year after year through routine, through fairly good or fairly bad, never quite realizing what we are experiencing, never seeing life as a whole, or any part of it, perhaps, in complete unity. Words, acts, sights, pass through our experience hazily, suggesting meanings which we never fully grasp. Grief and love, the most intense, perhaps, of sensations, we seldom understand except by comparison with what has been said of the grief and love of others. Happiness remains at best a diffused emotion —felt, but not comprehended. Thought, if in some moment of intense clarity it grasps our relationship to the stream of life, in the next shreds into trivialities. Is this true? Test it by any experience that is still fresh in memory. See how dull, by comparison with the vivid colors of the scene itself, are even now your ideas of what it meant to you, how obscure its relations to your later life. The moment you fell in love, the hour after your child had died, the instant when you reached the peak, the quarrel that began a misunderstanding not yet ended, the subtle household strain that pulls apart untiringly though it never sunders two who love each other—all these I challenge you to define, to explain, to lift into the light above the turbid sea of complex currents which is life.

And this, of course, is what good poetry does. It seizes the moment, the situation, the thought; drags it palpitating from life and flings it, quivering with its own rhythmic movement, into expression. The thing cannot be done in mere prose, for there is more than explanation to the process. The words themselves, in their color and suggestiveness, the rhythms that carry them, contribute to the sense, even as overtones help to make the music.

All this may sound a little exalted to the comfortable general reader, who does not often deal in such intense commodities as death and love. And yet I have mentioned nothing that does not at one time or another, and frequently rather than the opposite, come into his life, and need, not constant, certainly, but at least occasional, interpretation. Death and love, and also friendship, jealousy, courage, self-sacrifice, hate—these cannot be avoided. We must experience them. So do the animals, who gain from their experiences blind, instinctive repulsions or unreasoning likes and distrusts. There are many ways of escaping from such a bovine acquiescence, content to have felt, not desirous to grasp and know and relate. Poetry, which clears and intensifies like a glass held upon a distant snowpeak, is one of the best.

But there is another service that poetry, among all writing, best renders to the general reader, *when he needs it;* a service less obvious, but sometimes, I think, more important. Poetry insures an extension of youth.

Men and women vary in their emotional susceptibility. Some go through life always clouded, always dull, like a piece of glass cut in semblance of a gem, that refracts no colors and is empty of light. Others are vivid, impressionable, reacting to every experience. Some of us are most aroused by contact with one another. Interest awakens at the sound of a voice; we

are most alive when most with our kind. Others, like
Thoreau, respond best in solitude. The veery thrush
singing dimly in the hemlocks at twilight moves them
more powerfully than a cheer. A deep meadow awave
with headed grass, a solemn hill shouldering the sky,
a clear blue air washing over the pasture slopes and
down among the tree-tops of the valley, thrills them
more than all the men in all the streets of the world.
It makes no difference. To every one, dull and vivid,
social and solitary, age brings its changes. We may
understand better, but the vividness is less, the emotions are tamer. They do not fully respond, as the
bell in the deserted house only half tinkles to our pulling.

> *Si jeunesse savait,*
> *Si vielliesse pouvait.*

But to be able comes before to know. We must
react to experiences before it is worth while to comprehend them. And after one is well enmeshed in
the routine of plodding life, after the freshness of the
emotions (and this is a definition of youth) is gone,
it is difficult to react. I can travel now, if I wish,
to the coral islands or the Spanish Main, but it is too
late.

Few willingly part with the fresh impressionability
of youth. Sometimes, as I have already suggested, the
faculties of sensation become atrophied, if indeed they
ever existed. I know no more dismal spectacle than
a man talking shop on a moonlit hill in August, a

woman gossipping by the rail of a steamer plunging through the sapphire of the Gulf Stream, or a couple perusing advertisements throughout a Beethoven symphony. I will not advance as typical a drummer I once saw read a cheap magazine from cover to cover in the finest stretch of the Canadian Rockies. He was not a man, but a sample-fed, word-emitting machine. These people, emotionally speaking, are senile. They should not try to read poetry.

But most of us—even those who are outwardly commonplace, practical, unenthusiastic, "solid," and not "sensitive"—lose our youthful keenness with regret. And that is why poetry, except for the hopelessly sodden, is a tonic worthy of a great price. For the right poetry at the right time has the indubitable power to stir the emotions that experience is no longer able to arouse. I cannot give satisfactory instances, for the reaction is highly personal. What with me stirs a brain cell long dormant to action will leave another unmoved, and vice versa. However, to make clear my meaning, let us take Romance, the kind that one capitalizes, that belongs to Youth, also capitalized, and dwells in Granada or Sicily or the Spanish Main. The middle-aged gentleman on a winter cruise for his jaded nerves cannot expect a thrill from sights alone. If it is not lost for him utterly, it is only because Keats has kept it, in—

> . . . Magic casements, opening on the foam
> Of perilous seas, in faery lands forlorn,

and Nashe in—

> Brightness falls from the air;
> Queens have died young and fair.

Or consider the joy of travel renewed in Kipling's—

> Then home, get her home, where the drunken rollers comb,
>   And the shouting seas drive by,
> And the engines stamp and ring, and the wet bows reel and
>   swing,
>   And the Southern Cross rides high!
> Yes, the old lost stars wheel back, dear lass,
>   That blaze in the velvet blue.

Or the multitudinous experiences of vivid life that crowd the pages of men like Shakespeare, or Chaucer, who thanked God that he had known his world as in his time. Even in these shopworn quotations the power still remains.

Somewhere in poetry, and best in poetry because there most concentrated and most penetrative, lies crystallized experience at hand for all who need it. It is not difficult to find, although no one can find it for you. It is not necessarily exalted, romantic, passionate; it may be comfortable, homely, gentle or hearty, vigorous and cheerful; it may be anything but commonplace, for no true emotion is ever commonplace. I have known men of one poet; and yet that poet gave them the satisfaction they required. I know others whose occasional dip into poetry leads to no rapture of beauty, no throbbing vision into eternity; and yet without poetry they would be less alive, their minds would be less young. As children, most of us would have flushed before the beauty of a sunrise on a tropic ocean, felt dimly if profoundly—and forgotten. The poet—like the painter—has caught, has interpreted, has preserved the experience, so that, like music, it may be renewed. And he can perform that miracle for greater things than sunrises. This, perhaps, is the best of all reasons why every one except the emotionally senile should sometimes read poetry.

I know at least one honest Philistine who, unlike many Philistines, has traveled through the Promised Land—and does not like it. When his emotional friends talk sentimentalism and call it literature, or his esthetic acquaintances erect affectations and call them art, he has the proper word of irony that brings them back to food, money, and other verities. His voice haunts me now, suggesting that, in spite of the reasons I have advanced, the general reader can scarcely be expected to read modern poetry, and that therefore his habit of skipping must continue. He would say that most modern poetry is unreadable, at least by the average man. He would say that if the infinitely complex study of emotional mind-states that lies behind the poetry of Edwin Arlington Robinson, or the eerie otherworldliness of Yeats, or the harsh virility of Sandburg is to be regarded as an intensification and clarification of experience, he begs to be excused. He would say that if the lyrics of subtle and passionate emotion and the drab stories of sex experience that make up so many pages of modern anthologies represent a renewal and extension of youth, it was not *his* youth. He prefers to be sanely old rather than erotically young. He will stick to the daily paper and flat prose.

Well, it is easy to answer him by ruling out modern poetry from the argument. There was more good poetry, neither complex, nor erotic, nor esoteric, written before our generation than even a maker of anthologies is likely to read. But I am not willing to dodge the issue so readily. There *is* modern poetry for every reader who is competent to read poetry at all. If there is none too much of it, that is his own fault. If there is much that makes no appeal to him, that is as it should be.

It is true that a very large proportion of contemporary poetry is well-nigh unintelligible to the gentleman whose reading, like his experience, does not often venture beyond the primitive emotions. Why should it not be? The modern lyric is untroubled by the social conscience. It is highly individual, for it is written by men of intense individuality for readers whose imaginations require an intimate appeal. Such minds demand poetry prevailingly, just as the average reader demands prose prevailingly. They profit by prose now and then, just as, occasionally, he profits by poetry. We talk so much of the enormous growth of the mass of average readers in recent years that we forget the corresponding growth in the number of individualities that are not average. Much modern poetry is written for such readers, for men and women whose minds are sensitive to intricate emotional experience, who can and do respond to otherworldliness, to the subtly romantic, the finely esthetic, and the intricately ideal. They deserve whatever poetry they may desire.

The important point to note is that they do not get it. It is they—far more than the Philistines—who complain that modern poetry is insufficient for their needs. The highly personal lyric is probably more perfected, more abundant, and more poignant in its appeal to living minds now than ever before in the history of our civilization. But it occupies only one province of poetry. A lover of poetry desires, far more keenly than the general reader, to have verse of his own day that is more Shakespearian, more Miltonic, more Sophoclean than this. He wants poetry that lifts spacious times into spacious verse, poetry that "enlumynes," like Petrarch's "rhetorike sweete," a race and a civilization. He desires, in addition to what he is already getting, precisely that poetry so universal in its subject-matter and its appeal, which the general reader thinks he would read if he found it instead of "lyrical subtleties" in his pages.

Well, they do not get it very abundantly to-day, let us admit the fact freely. But the fault is not altogether the poets'. The fault is in the intractable mediocrity of the age, which resists transference into poetry as stiff clay resists the hoe of the cultivator. The fault lies in the general reader himself, whose very opposition to poetry because it *is* poetry makes him a difficult person to write for. Commercialized minds, given over to convention, denying their sentiment and idealism, or wasting them upon cheap and meretricious literature, do not make a good audience. Our few poets in English who have possessed some universality of appeal have had to make concessions. Kipling has been the most popular among good English poets in our time; but he has had to put journalism into much of his poetry in order to succeed. And Kipling is not read so much as a certain American writer who discovered that by writing verse in prose form he could make the public forget their prejudice against poetry and indulge their natural pleasure in rhythm and rime.

A striking proof of all that I have been writing is to be found in so-called magazine verse. Sneers at magazine poetry are unjust because they are unintelligent. It is quite true that most of it consists of the highly individualistic lyric of which I have spoken above. But in comparison with the imaginative prose of the typical popular magazine, it presents a most instructive contrast. The prose is too frequently sensational or sentimental, vulgar or smart. The verse, even though narrow in its appeal, and sometimes slight, is at least excellent in art, admirable in execution, and vigorous and unsentimental in tone. Regarded as literature, it is very much more satisfactory than the bulk of magazine prose. Indeed, there is less difference between the best and the worst of our magazines than between the verse and the prose in any one of them.

And if this verse is too special in its subject-matter to be altogether satisfactory, if so little of it appeals to the general reader, is it not his fault? He neglects the poetry from habit rather than from conviction based on experience. Because he skips it, and has skipped it until habit has become a convention, much of it has become by natural adaptation of supply to demand too literary, too narrow, too subtle and complex for him now. The vicious circle is complete.

This circle may soon be broken. A ferment, which in the 'nineties stirred in journalism, and a decade later transformed our drama, is working now in verse. The poetical revival now upon us may be richer so far in promise than in great poetry, but it is very significant. For one thing, it is advertising poetry, and since poetry is precisely what Shakespeare called it, caviare to the general—a special commodity for occasional use—a little advertising will be good for it. Again, the verse that has sprung from the movement is much of it thoroughly interesting. Some of it is as bizarre as the new art of the futurists and the vorticists; some is merely vulgar, some merely affected, some hopelessly obscure; but other poems, without convincing us of their greatness, seem as original and creative as were Browning and Whitman in their day. Probably, like the new painting, the movement is more significant than the movers.

Nevertheless, if one is willing to put aside prejudice, suspend judgment, and look ahead, *vers libre,* even when more *libre* than *vers,* is full of meaning—poetic realism, even when more real than poetry, charged with possibility. For with all its imperfections much of this new poetry is trying to mean more than ever before to the general reader. I am not sure that the democracy can be interpreted for him in noble poetry and remain the democracy he knows. And yet I think, and I believe, that, in his sub-consciousness at least, he feels an intense longing to find the everyday life in which we all live—so thrilling beneath the surface—interpreted, swung into that rhythmic significance that will make it part of the vast and flowing stream of all life. I can tolerate many short, rough words in poetry, and much that we have been accustomed to regard as prose, on the way to such a goal.

For I honestly believe that it is better to read fantastic poetry, coarse poetry, prosaic poetry—anything but vulgar and sentimental poetry—than no poetry at all. To be susceptible to no revival of the vivid emotions of youth, to be touched by no thoughts more intense than our own, to be accessible to no imaginative interpretation of the life we lead—this seems to me to be a heavy misfortune. But to possess, as most of us do, our share of all these qualities, and then at no time, in no fitting mood or proffered opportunity, to read poetry—this can only be regarded as deafness by habit and blindness from choice.

Eye, Ear, and Mind

OUR eyes are more civilized than our ears, and much more civilized than our minds; that is the flat truth, and it accounts for a good deal that puzzles worthy people who wish to reform literature.

Consider the musical comedy of the kind that runs for a year and costs the price of two books for a good seat. Its humor is either good horseplay or vulgar farce, and its literary quality nil. Its music is better, less banal than the words, and, sometimes, almost excellent. But its setting, the costumes, the scenic effects, the stage painting, and, most of all, the color schemes are always artistic and sometimes exquisite. They intrigue the most sophisticated taste, which is not surprising; yet, at the same time, the multitude likes them, pays for them, stays away if they are not right. Eye is an esthete, ear is, at least, cultivated, mind is a gross barbarian, unwilling to think, and desirous only of a tickle or a prod.

Or to localize the scene and change the angle a trifle, compare the New York ear for music with the New York taste for reading. The audiences who hear good concerts, good operas, good oratorios, and thoroughly appreciate them, far outrun in number the readers of equally artistic or intellectual books. Ear is more cultivated than mind, musical appreciation keener than literary taste. A good stage set on a first night in this same metropolis of the arts, will get a round of applause, when not only often, but usually, perfection of lines, or poignancy of thought in the dialogue, will miss praise altogether. Eye detects sheer beauty instantly, mind lags or is dull to it.

This is a fact; the cause of it let psychologists explain, as they can, of course, very readily. It is a rather encouraging fact, for it seems to indicate that our members educate themselves one at a time, and yet, as parts of a single body corporate, must help each other's education. If we grow critical of the sped-up background of a movie scene, we may grow critical of its sped-up plot. Eye may teach the ear, ear lift the mind to more strenuous intellectual efforts.

And, of course, it explains why the literary reformers have such difficulties with the multitude. Why, they say, do these women, whose dress is admirably designed and colored, whose living rooms are proportioned and furnished in taste, who know good music from bad, and enjoy the former—why do they read novels without the least distinction, without beauty or truth, barely raised above vulgarity? Why, they say, does this man who coöperates with his architect in the building of a country house which would have been a credit to any period, who is a connoisseur in wine and cigars, and unerring in his judgment of pictures, why does he definitely prefer the commonplace in literature? Eye, ear, and tongue are civilized; intellect remains a gross feeder still.   Good reading comes last among the arts of taste.

This is not an essay in reform; it is content to be a question mark; but one bit of preaching may slip in at the end.   Why give eye and ear all the fine experiences?   Why not do something for poor, slovenly mind?   The truth is that we are lazy.   In a stage full of shimmering beauty, in a concert of chamber music, in a fine building, or an admirable sketch, others do the work, we have only to gaze or listen in order to pluck some, at least, of the fruits of art.   But fine novels take fine reading; fine essays take fine thinking; fine poetry takes fine feeling.   We balk at the effort, and ask, like the audience at the movies, that eye should take the easier way.   And hence the American reader still faintly suggests the Fiji Islander, who wears a silk hat and patent leathers on a tattooed naked body.

For all we can tell, that may be the direction of Progress.   In 2021 New Yorkers may be gazing at a city beautiful, where even the subways give forth sweet sounds; and reading novelized movies in words of one syllable.   Eye may win the race and starve out the other members.   It would be a bad future for publishers and authors; and I am against it, even as a possibility.   Hence my energies will be devoted to poking, thrilling, energizing, tonicking that lazy old organism, half asleep still—Mind.

Out with the Dilettante

A few years ago drums and trumpets in American magazines and publishers' advertisements announced that the essay was coming to its own again. We were to vary our diet of short stories with pleasing disquisitions, to find in books of essays a substitute for the volume of sermons grown obsolete, and to titillate our finer senses by graceful prose that should teach us without didacticism, and present contemporary life without the incumbrance of a plot.

The promise was welcome. American literature has been at its very best in the essay. In the essay, with few exceptions, it has more often than elsewhere attained world-wide estimation. Emerson, Thoreau, Oliver Wendell Holmes were primarily essayists. Hawthorne and Irving were essayists as much as romancers. Franklin was a common sense essayist. Jonathan Edwards will some day be presented (by excerpt) as a moral essayist of a high order. And there was Lowell.

Have they had worthy successors? In the years after the Civil War certainly none of equal eminence. But it is too early to say that the trumpets and drums of the last decade were false heralds. The brilliant epithets of Chesterton, the perfect sophistication of Pearsall Smith (an American, but expatriated), the placid depth of Hudson's nature studies, are not paralleled on this side of the water, yet with Crothers, Gerould, Repplier, Colby, Morley, Strunsky, we need not fear comparison in the critical genre, unless it be with the incomparable Max Beerbohm.

Two kinds of expository writing are natural for Americans. The first is a hard-hitting statement, straight out of intense feeling or labored thought. That was Emerson's way (in spite of his expansiveness), and Thoreau's also. You read them by pithy sentences, not paragraphs. They assail you by ideas, not by insidious structures of thought. The second is an easy-going comment on life, often slangy or colloquial and frequently so undignified as not to seem literature. Mark Twain and Josh Billings wrote that way; Ring Lardner writes so to-day.

When the straight-from-the-shoulder American takes time to finish his thought, to mold his sentences, to brain his reader with a perfect expression of his tense emotion, then he makes literature. And when the easy-going humorist, often nowadays a column conductor, or a contributor to *The Saturday Evening Post,* takes time to deepen his observation and to say it with real words instead of worn symbols, he makes, and does make, literature. More are doing it than the skeptical realize. The new epoch of the American essay is well under way.

But the desire to "make literature" in America is too often wasted. The would-be essayist wastes it in pretty writing about trivial things—neighbors' back yards, books I have read, the idiosyncrasies of cats, humors of the streets—the sort of dilettantish comment that older nations writing of more settled, richer civilizations can do well—that Anatole France and occasional essayists of *Punch* or *The Spectator* can do well and most of us do indifferently. We are a humorous people, but not a playful one. Light irony is not our forte. Strength and humorous exaggeration come more readily to our pens than grace. We are better inspired by the follies of the crowd, or the errors of humanity, than by the whims of culture or aspects of pleasant leisure. And when we try to put on style in the manner of Lamb or Hazlitt, Stevenson or Beerbohm, we seldom exceed the second rate.

When the newspaper and magazine humorists of democracy learn to write better; when the moralists and reformers and critics of American life learn to mature and perfect their thought until what they write is as good as their intentions—then the trumpets and drums may sound again, and with justification. Many have; may others follow.

And perhaps then we can scrap a mass of fine writing about nothing in particular, that calls itself the American literary essay, and yet is neither American in inspiration, native in style, nor good for anything whatsoever, except exercise in words. Out with the dilettantes. We are tired of the merely literary; we want real literature in the essay as elsewhere.

Flat Prose

SOME time ago a writer protested against the taboo
on "beautiful prose." He asserted that the usual organs of publication, especially in America, reject with
deadly certainty all contributions whose style suggests
that melodious rhythm which De Quincey and Ruskin
made fashionable for their generations, and Stevenson
revived in the 'nineties. He complained that the writer
is no longer allowed to write as well as he can; that
he must abstract all unnecessary color of phrase, all
warmth of connotation and grace of rhythm from his
style, lest he should seem to be striving for "atmosphere," instead of going about his proper business,
which is to fill the greedy stomach of the public with
facts.

Unfortunately, this timely fighter in a good cause
was too enamored of the art whose suppression he was
bewailing. He so far forgot himself as to make his
own style "beautiful" in the old-time fashion, and thus
must have roused the prejudice of the multitude, who
had to study such style in college, and knew from sad
experience that it takes longer to read than the other
kind.

But there are other and safer ways of combating
the taste for flat prose. One might be to print parallel
columns of "newspaper English" (which they threaten

now to teach in the schools) until the eye sickened of its deadly monotony. This is a bad way. The average reader would not see the point. Paragraphs from a dozen American papers, all couched in the same utilitarian dialect,—simple but not always clear, concise yet seldom accurate, emphatic but as ugly as the clank of an automobile chain,—why, we read thousands of such lines daily! We think in such English; we talk in it; to revolt from this style, to which the Associated Press has given the largest circulation on record, would be like protesting against the nitrogen in our air.

Books and magazines require a different reckoning. The author is still allowed to let himself go occasionally in books—especially in sentimental books. But the magazines, with few exceptions, have shut down the lid, and are keeping the stylistic afflatus under strict compression. No use to show them what they might publish if, with due exclusion of the merely pretty, the sing-song, and the weakly ornate, they were willing to let a little style escape. With complete cowardice, they will turn the general into the particular, and insist that in any case they will not publish *you*. Far better, it seems to me, to warn editors and the "practical public" as to what apparently is going to happen if ambitious authors are tied down much longer to flat prose.

It is not generally known, I believe, that post-impressionism has escaped from the field of pictorial art, and is running rampant in literature. At present, Miss Gertrude Stein is the chief culprit. Indeed, she may be called the founder of a coterie, if not of a school.

Her art has been defined recently by one of her admirers, who is also the subject, or victim, of the word-portrait from which I intend later to quote in illustration of my argument. "Gertrude Stein," says Miss Dodge, "is doing with words what Picasso is doing with paint. She is impelling language to induce new states of consciousness, and in doing so language becomes with her a creative art rather than a mirror of history." This, being written in psychological and not in post-impressionist English, is' fairly intelligible. But it does not touch the root of the matter. Miss Stein, the writer continues, uses "words that appeal to her as having the meaning they *seem* to have [that is, if "diuturnity" suggests a tumble downstairs, it *means* a tumble downstairs]. To present her impressions she chooses words for their inherent quality rather than their accepted meaning."

Let us watch the creative artist at her toil. The title of this particular word-picture is "Portrait of Mabel Dodge at the Villa Curonia." As the portrait itself has a beginning, but no middle, and only a faintly indicated end, I believe—though in my ignorance of just what it all means I am not sure—that I can quote at random without offense to the impressions derivable from the text.

Here then are a few paragraphs where the inherent quality of the words is said to induce new states of consciousness:—

"Bargaining is something and there is not that success. The intention is what if application has that accident results are reappearing. They did not darken. That was not an adulteration. . . . There is that particular half of directing that there is that particular whole direction that is not all the measure of any combination. Gliding is not heavily moving. Looking is not vanishing. Laughing is not evaporation.

"Praying has intention and relieving that situation is not solemn. There comes that way.

"There is all there is when there has all there has where there is what there is. That is what is done when there is done what is done and the union is won and the division is the explicit visit. There is not all of any visit."

After a hundred lines of this I wish to scream, I wish to burn the book, I am in agony. It is not because I know that words *cannot* be torn loose from their meanings without insulting the intellect. It is not because I see that this is a prime example of the "confusion of the arts." No, my feeling is purely physical. Some one has applied an egg-beater to my brain.

But having calmed myself by a sedative of flat prose from the paper, I realize that Miss Stein is more sinned against than sinning. She is merely a red flag waved by the *Zeitgeist*.

For this is the sort of thing we are bound to get if the lid is kept down on the stylists much longer. Repression has always bred revolt. Revolt breeds extravagance. And extravagance leads to absurdity. And yet even in the absurd, a sympathetic observer may detect a purpose which is honest and right. Miss

Stein has indubitably written nonsense, but she began with sense. For words *have* their sound-values as well as their sense-values, and prose rhythms *do* convey to the mind emotions that mere denotation cannot give. Rewrite the solemn glory of Old Testament diction in the flat colorless prose which just now is demanded, and wonder at the difference. Translate "the multitudinous seas incarnadine" into "making the ocean red,"—or, for more pertinent instances, imagine a Carlyle, an Emerson, a Lamb forced to exclude from his vocabulary every word not readily understood by the multitude, to iron out all whimseys, all melodies from his phrasing, and to plunk down his words one after the other in the order of elementary thought!

I am willing to fight to the last drop of ink against any attempt to bring back "fine writing" and ornate rhetoric into prose. "Expression is the dress of thought," and plain thinking and plain facts look best in simple clothing. Nevertheless, if we must write our stories, our essays, our novels, and (who knows) our poems in the flat prose of the news column,—if the editors will sit on the lid,—well, the public will get what it pays for, but sooner or later the spirit of style will ferment, will work, will grow violent under restraint. There will be reaction, explosion, revolution. The public will get its flat prose, and—in addition—not one, but a hundred Gertrude Steins.

VI
Men and Their Books

Conrad and Melville

THE appearance of the definitive edition of Joseph Conrad, with his interesting critical prefaces included, was a provocation to read and reread his remarkable series of books, the most remarkable contribution to English literature by an alien since the language began. But is it a reason for writing more of an author already more discussed than any English stylist of our time? For myself, I answer, yes, because I have found no adequate definition of the difference between Conrad and us to whom English thinking is native, nor a definition of his place, historically considered, in the modern scheme; no definition, that is, which explains my own impressions of Conrad. And therefore I shall proceed, as all readers should, to make my own.

If you ask readers why they like Conrad, two out of three will answer, because he is a great stylist, or because he writes of the sea. I doubt the worth of such answers. Many buy books because they are written by great stylists, but few read for just that reason. They read because there is something in an author's work which attracts them to his style, and that something may be study of character, skill in narrative, or profundity in truth, of which style is the perfect expression, but not the thing itself. Only connoisseurs, and few of them, read for style. And, furthermore, I very much doubt whether readers go to Conrad to learn about the sea. They might learn as much from Cooper or Melville, but they have not gone there much of late. And many an ardent lover of Conrad would rather be whipped than go from New York to Liverpool on a square-rigged ship.

In any case, these answers, which make up the sum of most writing about Conrad, do not define him. To say that an author is a stylist is about as helpful as to say that he is a thinker. And Conrad would have had his reputation if he had migrated to Kansas instead of to the English sea.

In point of fact, much may be said, and with justice, against Conrad's style. It misses occasionally the English idiom, and sometimes English grammar, which is a trivial criticism. It offends more frequently against the literary virtues of conciseness and economy, which is not a trivial criticism. Conrad, like the writers of Elizabethan prose (whom he resembles in ardency and in freshness), too often wraps you in words, stupefies you with gorgeous repetition, goes about and about and about, trailing phrases after him, while the procession of narrative images halts. He can be as prolix in his brooding descriptions as Meredith with his intellectual vaudeville. Indeed, many give him lip service solely because they like to be intoxicated, to be carried away, by words. A slight change of taste, such as that which has come about since Meredith was on every one's tongue, will make such defects manifest. Meredith lives in spite of his prolixities, and so will Conrad, but neither because they are perfect English stylists.

I am sure also that Conrad, at his very best, is not so good as Melville, at his best, in nautical narrative; as Melville in, say, the first day of the final chase of Moby Dick; I question whether he is as good in sea narrative as Cooper in the famous passage of Paul Jones's ship through the shoals. Such comparisons are, of course, rather futile. They differentiate among excellences, where taste is a factor. Nevertheless, it is belittling to a man who, above almost all others in our language, has brooded upon the mysteries of the mind's action, to say that he is great because he describes so well the sea.

We must seek elsewhere for a definition of the peculiar qualities of Conrad. And without a definition it is easy to admire but hard to estimate and understand him.

I believe, first of all, that Conrad has remained much more a Slav than he, or any of us, have been willing to admit. A friend of mine, married to a Slav, told me of her husband, how, with his cab at the door, and dinner waiting somewhere, he would sit brooding (so he said) over the wrongs of his race. It is dangerous to generalize in racial characteristics, but no one will dispute a tendency to brood as a characteristic of the Slav. The Russian novels are full of characters who brood, and of brooding upon the characters and their fates. The structure of the Russian story is determined not by events so much as by the results of passionate brooding upon the situation in which the imagined characters find themselves.

So it is with Conrad, always and everywhere. In "Nostromo" he broods upon the destructive power of a fixed idea; in "The Rescue" upon the result of flinging together elemental characters of the kind that life keeps separate; in "Youth" upon the illusions, more real than reality, of youth. No writer of our race had ever the patience to sit like an Eastern mystic over his scene, letting his eye fill with each slightest detail of it, feeling its contours around and above and beneath, separating each detail of wind and water, mood and emotion, memory and hope, and returning again and again to the task of description, until every impression was gathered, every strand of motive threaded to its source.

Henry James, you will say, was even more patient. Yes, but James did not brood. His work was active analysis, cutting finer and finer until the atom was reached. His mind was Occidental. He wished to know why the wheels went round. Conrad's, in this respect, is Oriental. He wants to see what things essentially are. Henry James refines but seldom repeats. Conrad, in such a story as "Gaspar Ruiz" for example, or in "Chance," gives the impression of not caring to understand if only he can fully picture the mind that his brooding imagination draws further and further from its sheath. It is incredible, to one who has not counted, how many times he raises the same situation to the light—the Garibaldean and Nostromo, Mrs.

Travers marveling at her knowledge of Lingard's heart
—turns it, opens it a little further, and puts it back
while he broods on. Here is the explanation of Conrad's prolixity; here the reason why among all living
novelists he is least a slave to incident, best able to
let his story grow as slowly as life, and still hold the
reader's interest. As we read Conrad we also brood;
we read slowly where elsewhere we read fast. Turns
of style, felicities of description, as of the tropic ocean,
or the faces of women, have their chance. And, of
course, the excellence, the charm of Conrad's style is
that in its nuances, its slow winding paragraphs, its
pausing sentences, and constant suggestion of depths
beyond depths, it is the perfect expression of the brooding mind that grasps its meaning by the repetition of
images that drop like pebbles, now here, now there,
in a fathomless pool.

This is to define Conrad in space, but not in time.
In time, he may be Slav or English, but certainly is
modern of the moderns. The tribute of admiration
and imitation from the youth of his own period alone
might prove this. But it is easier to prove than to
describe his modernity. To say that he takes the imagination afield into the margins of the world, where life
still escapes standardization and there are fresh aspects
of beauty, is to fail to differentiate him from Kipling
or Masefield. To say that he strikes below the act
and the will into realms of the sub-conscious, and
studies the mechanism as well as the results of emotion,
is but to place him, where indeed he belongs, among

the many writers who have learned of Henry James or moved in parallels beside him.

To get a better perspective of Conrad's essential modernity I should like to propose a more cogent comparison, and a more illuminating contrast, with a man whose achievements were in Conrad's own province, who challenges and rewards comparison, Herman Melville.

It may be that others have set "Moby Dick" beside the works of Conrad. Some one must have done it, so illuminating in both directions is the result. Here are two dreamers who write of the sea and strange men, of the wild elements and the mysterious in man; two authors who, a half century apart, sail the same seas and come home to write not so much of them as what they dream when they remember their experiences. Each man, as he writes, transcends the sea, sublimates it into a vapor of pure imagination, in which he clothes his idea of man, and so doing gives us not merely great literature, but sea narrative and description unsurpassed:

And thus, through the serene tranquillities of the tropical seas, among waves whose hand-clappings were suspended by exceeding rapture, Moby Dick moved on, still withholding from sight the full terrors of his submerged trunk, entirely hiding the wretched hideousness of his jaw.

Melville, writer of vivid descriptions of the South Seas, "Typee," "Omoo," which were perfect of their kind, but still only superlative travel books, distinguished in style but seldom lifting beyond autobiography, began another reminiscent narrative in "Moby Dick." In spite of his profound intellectual growth away from the cool and humorous youth who paddled the Marquesan lake with primitive beauties beside him, he seems to have meant in "The White Whale" to go back to his earlier manner, to write an accurate though highly personal account of the whaler's life, and to that end had assembled a mass of information upon the sperm whale to add to his own memories. Very literally the story begins as an autobiography; even the elemental figure of the cannibal, Queequeg, with his incongruous idol and harpoon in a New Bedford lodging house, does not warn of what is to come. But even before the *Pequod* leaves sane Nantucket an undercurrent begins to sweep through the narrative. This brooding captain, Ahab (for Melville also broods, though with characteristic difference), and his ivory leg, those warning voices in the mist, the strange crew of all races and temperaments—the civilized, the barbarous, and the savage—in their ship, which is a microcosm, hints that creep in of the white whale whose nature is inimical to man and arouses passions deeper than gain or revenge—all this prepares the reader for something more than incident. From the mood of Defoe one passes, by jerks and reversions, to the atmosphere of "The Ancient Mariner" and of "Manfred."

When Conrad could not manage his story he laid

it aside, sometimes for twenty years, as with "The Rescue." But Melville was a wilder soul, a greater man, and probably a greater artist, but a lesser craftsman. He lost control of his book. He loaded his whaling story with casks of natural history, deck loaded it with essays on the moral nature of man, lashed to its sides dramatic dialogues on the soul, built up a superstructure of symbolism and allegory, until the tale foundered and went down, like the *Pequod*. And then it emerged again a dream ship searching for a dream whale, manned by fantastic and terrible dreams; and every now and then, as dreams will, it takes on an appearance of reality more vivid than anything in life, more real than anything in Conrad—the meeting with the *Rachel* and her captain seeking his drowned son, the rising of Moby Dick with the dead Parsee bound to his terrible flank, the grim dialogues of Ahab. . . .

In this bursting of bounds, in these epic grandeurs in the midst of confusion, and vivid realities mingled with untrammeled speculation, lies the secret of Melville's purpose, and, by contrast, the explanation of Conrad's modern effect beside him. Melville, friend of Hawthorne and transcendentalist philosopher on his own account, sees nature as greater and more terrible than man. He sees the will of man trying to control the universe, but failing; crushed if uncowed by the unmeasured power of an evil nature, which his little spirit, once it loses touch with the will of God, vainly encounters. Give man eyes only in the top of his head, looking heavenward, says Ahab, urging the blacksmith, who makes him a new leg buckle, to forge a new creature complete. He writes of man at the beginning of the age of science, aware of the vast powers of material nature, fretting that his own body is part of them, desirous to control them by mere will, fighting his own moral nature as did Ahab in his insensate pursuit of Moby Dick, and destroyed by his own ambitions, even as Ahab, the *Pequod,* and all her crew went down before the lashings and charges of the white whale.

"Oh, Life," says Ahab, "here I am, proud as a Greek god, and yet standing debtor to this blockhead [the carpenter] for a bone to stand on! . . . I owe for the flesh in the tongue I brag with." And yet as they approach the final waters "the old man's purpose intensified itself. His firm lips met like the lips of a vise; the Delta of his forehead's veins swelled like overladen brooks; in his very sleep his ringing cry ran through the vaulted hull: 'Stern all! The white whale spouts thick blood!'"

Conrad comes at the height of the age of science. The seas for him are full of dark mysteries, but these mysteries are only the reflections of man. Man dominates the earth and sea, man conquers the typhoon, intelligent man subdues the savage wills of the barbarians of the shallows, man has learned to master all but his own heart. The center of gravity shifts from without to within. The philosopher, reasoning of God and of nature, gives place to the psychologist brooding over an organism that is seat of God and master of the elements. Melville is centrifugal, Conrad centripetal. Melville's theme is too great for him; it breaks his story, but the fragments are magnificent. Conrad's task is easier because it is more limited; his theme is always in control. He broods over man in a world where nature has been conquered, although the mind still remains inexplicable. The emphasis shifts from external symbols of the immensities of good and evil to the behavior of personality under stress. Melville is a moral philosopher, Conrad a speculative psychologist.

The essentially modern quality of Conrad lies in this transference of wonder from nature to the behavior of man, the modern man for whom lightning is only electricity and wind the relief of pressure from hemisphere to hemisphere. Mystery lies in the personality now, not in the blind forces that shape and are shaped by it. It is the difference, in a sense, between Hawthorne, who saw the world as shadow and illusion, symbolizing forces inimical to humanity, and Hardy, who sees in external nature the grim scientific fact of environment. It is a difference between eras more marked in Conrad than in many of his contemporaries, because, like Melville, Hawthorne, and Poe, he avoids the plain prose of realism and sets his romantic heroes against the great powers of nature—tempests, the earthquake, solitude, and grandeur. Thus the contrast is marked by the very resemblance of romantic setting. For Conrad's tempests blow only to beat upon the mind whose behavior he is studying;

his moral problems are raised only that he may study their effect upon man.

If, then, we are to estimate Conrad's work, let us begin by defining him in these terms. He is a Slav who broods by racial habit as well as by necessity of his theme. He is a modern who accepts the growing control of physical forces by the intellect and turns from the mystery of nature to brood upon personality. From this personality he makes his stories. External nature bulks large in them, because it is when beat upon by adversity, brought face to face with the elemental powers, and driven into strange efforts of will by the storms without that man's personality reaches the tensest pitch. Plot of itself means little to Conrad and that is why so few can tell with accuracy the stories of his longer novels. His characters are concrete. They are not symbols of the moral nature, like Melville's men, but they are nevertheless phases of personality and therefore they shift and dim from story to story, like lanterns in a wood. Knowing their hearts to the uttermost, and even their gestures, one nevertheless forgets sometimes their names, the ends to which they come, the tales in which they appear. The same phase, indeed, appears under different names in several stories.

Melville crossed the shadow line in his pursuit of the secret of man's relation to the universe; only magnificent fragments of his imagination were salvaged for his books. Conrad sails on an open sea, tamed by wireless and conquered by steel. Mystery for him lies not beyond the horizon, but in his fellow passengers. On them he broods. His achievement is more complete than Melville's; his scope is less. When the physicists have resolved, as apparently they soon will do, this earthy matter where now with our implements and our machinery we are so much at home, into mysterious force as intangible as will and moral desire, some new transcendental novelist will assume Melville's task. The sea, earth, and sky, and the creatures moving therein again will become symbols, and the pursuit of Moby Dick be renewed. But now, for a while, science has pushed back the unknown to the horizon and given us a little space of light in the darkness of the universe. There the ego is for a time the greatest mystery. It is an opportunity for the psychologists and, while we are thinking less of the soul, they have rushed to study the mechanics of the brain. It was Conrad's opportunity also to brood upon the romance of personality at the moment of man's greatest victory over dark external force.

The Novelist of Pity

To those interested in the meaning of the generation
that has now left us quivering on the beach of after
war, Thomas Hardy's books are so engrossing that to
write of them needs no pretext; yet the recent publication of an anniversary edition with all his prefaces included is a welcome excuse for what I propose to make,
not so much an essay as a record of a sudden understanding.   Long familiarity with Hardy's novels had
led to an afternoon of conversation with the author
himself in the mildness of old age.   But he remained
for me a still inexplicable figure, belonging to an earlier
century, yet in other respects so clearly abreast, if not
ahead, of the emotions of our own times, that at eighty
he saw the young men beginning to follow him.   It was
a reading of "The Dynasts," in the tall, red volumes of
the new edition, that suddenly and unexpectedly
seemed to give me a key.

The danger, so I had thought and think, is that
Hardy bids fair to become a legendary figure with an
attribute, as is the way with such figures, better known
than the man himself.   "Hardy, oh, yes, the pessimist"
threatens to become all the schoolboy knows and all
he needs to know of him, and his alleged philosophy
of gloom is already overshadowing the man's intense
interest in strong and appealing life.   It has been the

fate of many a great artist to get a nickname, like a boy, and never be rid of it.

I do not wish by any ingenious fabrication to prove that Hardy was not a pessimist. He is the father of the English school that refuse to be either deists or moralists, and, like them, pushes his stories to an end that is often bitter. His temperament is cast in that brooding, reflective mood that concerns itself less readily with jollity than with grief, and is therefore ever slanting toward pessimism. This, even his style indicates. Like the somber Hawthorne's, his style is brooding, adumbrative, rather than incisive or brilliant, and it often limps among the facts of his story like a man in pain. Indeed, Hardy is seldom a stylist, except when his mood is somber; therefore it is by his sadder passages that we remember him. Yet the most important fact about Hardy is not that he is pessimistic.

His manner of telling a story, however, helps to confirm the popular impression. Hardy's plots are a series of accidents, by which the doom of some lovely or aspiring spirit comes upon it by the slow drift of misfortune. Tess, Grace, Eustacia, Jude—it is clear enough to what joys and sorrows their natures make them liable. But the master prepares for them trivial error, unhappy coincidence, unnecessary misfortune, until it is not surprising if the analytic mind insists that he is laboring some thesis of pessimism to be worked out by concrete example.

Nevertheless, this is incomplete definition, and it is annoying that the dean of letters in our tongue should be subjected to a sophomoric formula in which the emphasis is wrongly placed. The critics, in general, have defined this pessimism, stopped there, and said, this is Hardy. But youth that does not like pessimism reads Hardy avidly. More light is needed.

Mr. Hardy himself does not suggest the simple and melancholy pessimist. A mild old man, gentleness is the first quality one feels in him, but at eighty he still waxed his mustache tips, and his eyes lit eagerly. I remember how earnestly he denied knowledge of science, piqued, I suppose, by the omniscient who had declared that his art consisted of applying the results of scientific inquiry to the study of simple human nature. If his treatment of nature was scientific, as I affirmed, his wife agreed, and he did not deny, then, he implied, his knowledge came by intuition, not by theory. The war was still on when I talked with him. It had lifted him to poetry at first, but by 1918 no longer interested him vitally. "It is too mechanical," he said. His novels, where fate seems to operate mechanically sometimes, he was willing that day to set aside as nil. Poetry, he thought, was the only proper form of expression. The novel was too indirect; too wasteful of time and space in its attempt to come at real issues. Yet these real issues, it appeared as we talked, were not theories. Ideas, he said, if emphasized, destroy art. Writers, he thought, in the future would give up pure fiction (serious writers, I suppose he meant). Poetry would be their shorthand; they would by intenser language cut short to their end.

What was *his* end? Not mechanical, scientific theories, that was clear. Not mere realistic description of life. He told me he had little faith in mere observation, except for comic or quaint characterization. He had seldom if ever studied a serious character from a model. One woman he invented entirely (was it Tess?) and she was thought to be his best. What, then, was this essence which the novelist, growing old, would convey now in concentrated form by poetry which to him, so he said, was story-telling in verse.

It is easier to understand what he meant if one thinks how definitely Hardy belongs to his age, the latter nineteenth century, in spite of his reachings forward. On the one hand, his very gentleness is characteristic of a period that was above all others humane. On the other, his somber moods sprang from a generation that was the first to understand the implications of the struggle for life in the animal world all about them. They, to be sure, deduced from what they saw a vague theory of evolution in which the best (who were themselves) somehow were to come out best in the end. He, though gentle as they were, deduced nothing so cheerful, saw rather the terrible discrepancies between fact and theory, so that his very gentleness made him pessimistic, where Browning was optimistic. Then, like Hawthorne in the generation before him, Hardy went back to an earlier, simpler life than his own, and there made his inquiries. Hawthorne, who did not accept the theology of Puritanism, was yet strangely troubled by the problem of sin.

Hardy, accepting the implacability of evolution without its easy optimism, was intensely moved to pity. This is his open secret.

The clearest statement is in his poetry, where again and again, in our conversation that day, he seemed to be placing it—most of all, I think, in "The Dynasts."

"The Dynasts" was published too soon. We English speakers, in 1904-1906, were beginning to read plays again, under the stimulus of a dramatic revival, and the plays we read were successful on the stage. As I recollect the criticism of "The Dynasts," much of it at least was busied with the form of the drama, its great length and unwieldiness. We thought of it not as a dramatic epic, but as a dramatized novel—a mistake. We thought that Hardy was taking the long way around, when in truth he had found a short cut to his issues. That "The Dynasts," considering the vastness of its Napoleonic subject, was far more concise, more direct, clearer than his novels, did not become manifest, although the sharper-eyed may have seen it.

In "The Dynasts" I find all of Hardy. The Immanent Will is God, as Hardy conceives Him, neither rational nor entirely conscious, frustrating His own seeming ends, without irony and without compassion, and yet perhaps evolving like His world, clearing like men's visions, moving towards consistency. The Sinister Angel and the Ironic Angel are moods well known to Hardy, but not loved by him. The Spirit of the Years that sees how poor human nature collides with accident, or the inevitable, and is bruised, is Hardy's reasoned philosophy. The Spirit of Pities (not always, as he says, logical or consistent) is Hardy's own desire, his will, his faint but deep-felt hope. I quote, from the very end of the great spectacle, some lines in which the Spirits, who have watched the confused tragedy of the Napoleonic age, sum up their thoughts:

AFTER SCENE

Spirit of the Years

Thus doth the Great Foresightless mechanize
Its blank entrancement now as evermore
Its ceaseless artistries in circumstance. . . .
Yet seems this vast and singular confection
Wherein our scenery glints of scantest size,
Inutile all—so far as reasonings tell.

Spirit of Pities

Thou arguest still the Inadvertent Mind.—
But, even so, shall blankness be for aye? . . .

Spirit of the Years

What wouldst have hoped and had the Will to be? . . .

Semi-chorus I of the Pities

Nay;—shall not Its blindness break?
Yea, must not Its heart awake,
          Promptly tending
          To Its mending
In a genial germing purpose, and for loving-kindness' sake?

Semi-chorus II

Should It never
Curb or cure
Aught whatever
Those endure
Whom It quickens, let them darkle to extinction swift and
sure.

Chorus

But—a stirring thrills the air
Like to sounds of joyance there
        That the rages
        Of the ages
Shall be cancelled, and deliverance offered from the darts
    that were,
Consciousness the Will informing, till It fashions all things
    fair!

The Spirit of the Years (which is another name for
Hardy's reflections upon life and history) planned in
sad conviction of the "blank entrancement" of the
Great Foresightless Will, those sad narratives in which
innocence, as in "Tess of the d'Ubervilles," is crushed,
or vivid personality frustrated, as in "The Return of
the Native." It is the Spirit of Pities in Hardy which
wrote the stories. Philosophy constructed them, but
pity worked them out.

The characters that Hardy loved—Grace, Marty
South, Jude, Tess—are life, brooding, intense, potential, and lovely, struggling against a fate which they

help to draw upon themselves, but which is, nevertheless, not necessary, not rational. The cruelty of this fate he assumes and depicts, but the stories are not told to describe it. It is his creatures that get the color, the interest; they are valuable to us, and would be to him, whatever the truth of his philosophy. But because he loves life, the living thing, even the lizard in the woods, he broods upon their frustrations.

Pessimistic Hardy is, as any gentle heart would be who chose to study misfortune; yet pessimist is not the right term for him. Realist he is clearly, in the philosophic sense of one who is willing to view things as they are without prejudice. I seek a term for a mild spirit who sees clearly that the sufferer is more intelligible than his fate, and so is pitiful even when most ruthless in the depiction of misfortune. Pity for the individual, not despair of the race, is his motive. And pity makes his gentle style, pity makes him regardless of artifice, and gives his often clumsy novels an undercurrent which sweeps them beyond technical masterpieces whose only merit is sharpness of thought. It is instructive to compare the relative fortunes of Hardy and Meredith, once always bracketed—the apostle of pity in comparison with the most subtle and brilliant mind of his time. Hardy has outranked him.

Already it begins to appear that the inconsistent, half-conscious Will that was the sum and substance of Hardy's pessimism was given certain attributes of gloom that scarcely belonged to it. The ruthless struggle for life by which the fittest for the circumstances of the moment, and by no means the best, survive at the expense of the others is no longer conceived as the clear law of human life. Science, with the rediscovery of Mendelism and its insistence upon psychological factors has submitted important qualifications to this deduction which Hardy, in common with others intellectually honest of his age, was forced to make. But it is not Hardy's philosophy, sound or unsound, that counts in his art, except in so far as it casts the plan of his stories, or sometimes, as in "Tess," or "The Woodlanders," gives too much play to cruel accident, and therefore an air of unreality to the tenser moments of the plots. Our critical emphasis in the past has been wrong. It should, to follow Hardy's own words, be set not upon the idea, the suggested explanation of misfortune, but upon the living creatures in his novels and poems alike. It is the characters he wrought in pity, and, it would appear, in hope, that make him a great man in our modern world, although only once did he pass beyond the bounds of his primitive Wessex. The novelist of pity and its poet, not the spokesman for pessimism, is the title I solicit for him.

Henry James

IT has always surprised Europeans that Henry James, the most intellectual of modern novelists, should have been an American; for most Europeans believe, as does Lowes Dickinson, that we are an intelligent but an unintellectual race. Was the fact so surprising after all? The most thoroughgoing pessimists come from optimistic communities. Henry James, considered as a literary phenomenon, represented a sensitive mind's reaction against the obviousness of the life that one finds in most American "best sellers." I suppose that he reacted too far. I feel sure of it when he is so unobvious that I cannot understand him. And yet every American writer must feel a little proud that there was one of our race who could make the great refusal of popularity, sever, with those intricate pen strokes of his, the bonds of interest that might have held the "general reader," and write just as well as he knew how.

Whether his novels and short stories gained by this heroic "highbrowism," is another question. Certainly they did not always do so. To get a million of readers is no sure sign of greatness; but to find only thousands, as did Henry James in his later books, is to be deplored. In "Daisy Miller" and "The Bostonians" he was a popular novelist of the best kind, a novelist who drew the best people to be his readers. But men read "The Golden Bowl" and "The Wings of the Dove" because they were skilful rather than because they were interesting. They were novelists' novels, like the professional matinées that "stars" give on Tuesday afternoons for the benefit of rivals and imitators in art.

But to stop here would be to misunderstand totally the greatest craftsman that has come out of America. The flat truth is that Henry James was not a novelist at all, at least in the good, old-fashioned sense that we usually give to the word. He was primarily a critic; the greatest American critic since Poe. Sometimes he criticized literature with supreme success, as in his "Notes on Novelists" of 1914; but ordinarily he criticized life. His later novels are one-fifth story, one-fifth character creation, and the rest pure criticism of life.

There is a curious passage in his "A Small Boy and Others"—the biography of the youth of William James and himself—telling how as a child in the hotels and resorts of Europe he spent his time in looking on at what was happening about him. He never got into the game very far, because he preferred to think about it. That is what Henry James did all his life long. He looked on, thought about life with that wonderfully keen, and subtle, and humorous mind of his, turned it into criticism; then fitted the results with enough plot to make them move,—and there was a so-called novel. Every one knows how in his last edition he rewrote some of his early stories to make them more subtle. It would have been amusing if he had seen fit to rewrite them altogether as critical essays upon international life! I wonder how much they would have suffered by the change.

This is why so many readers have been very proud of Henry James, and yet unable to defend him successfully against critics who pulled out handfuls of serpentine sentences from his latest novel, asking, "Do you call this fiction?" It was not fiction, not fiction at least as she used to be written; it was subtle, graceful, cunning analysis of life. Fiction is synthesis— building up, making a Becky Sharp, inventing a Meg Merrilies, constructing a plot. Criticism is analysis— taking down. Henry James was not so good at putting together as at taking to pieces. He was able in one art, but in the other he was great.

The current tendency to make every new figure in world literature conform to Greatness of a recognized variety or be dismissed, is unfortunate and misleading. We are to be congratulated that the greatness of Henry James was of a peculiar and irregular kind, a keen, inventing greatness, American in this if in nothing else. Unnumbered writers of the day, of whom Mr. Kipling is not the least eminent, have profited by his influence, and learned from him to give the final, subtle thought its final form. If that form in his own case was tortuous, intricate, difficult, why so was the thought. If it makes hard reading, his subject at least got hard thinking. Before you condemn that curious style of his—so easy to parody, so hard to imitate—

ask whether such refinement of thought as his could be much more simply expressed. Sometimes he could have been simpler, undoubtedly; it was his fault that he did not care to be; but that "plain American" would usually have served his purpose, is certainly false.

Henry James must yield first honors as a novelist, it may be, to others of his century if not of his generation. As a writer, above all as a writer of fine, imaginative criticism of the intellect as it moves through the complexities of modern civilization, he yields to no one of our time. Whether he has earned his distinction as an American writer I do not know, although I am inclined to believe that he is more American than the critics suspect; but as a master of English, and as a great figure in the broad sweep of international English literature, his place is secure.

The Satiric Rage of Butler

SAMUEL BUTLER's "Erewhon" has passed safely into the earthly paradise of the so-called classics. It has been recommended by distinguished men of letters, reprinted and far more widely read than on its first appearance; it has passed, by quotation and reference, into contemporary literature, and been taught in college classes. "Erewhon Revisited," written thirty years after "Erewhon," is less well known.

Mr. Moreby Acklom (whose name, let me assure the suspicious reader, is his own and not an Erewhonian inversion), in a most informing preface to a new edition, makes two assertions which may serve as my excuse for again endeavoring to explain the fascination for our generation of the work of Samuel Butler. College professors, he avers, have an antipathy for Samuel Butler; the chief interest of Butler, he further states, was in theology. Now I am a college professor without antipathy to Samuel Butler, with, on the contrary, the warmest admiration for his sardonic genius. And furthermore Butler's antipathy for college professors, which is supposed to have drawn their fire in return, is based upon a ruling passion far deeper than his accidental interest in theology, a passion that gives the tone and also the key to the best of his writings and which brought him into conflict with the "vested interests" of his times. It is his passion for honest thinking. If Butler's mark had been theology merely, his books would have passed with the interest in his target. He would be as difficult reading to-day as Swift in his "Tale of a Tub."

Like most of the great satirists of the world, Butler's *saeva indignatio* was aroused by the daily conflicts between reason and stupidity, between candor and disingenuousness, with all their mutations of hypocrisy, guile, deceit, and sham. In "Erewhon" it was human unreason, as a clever youth sees it, that he was attacking. We remember vividly the beautiful Erewhonians, who knew disease to be sin, but believed vice to be only disease. We remember the "straighteners" who gave moral medicine to the ethically unwell, the musical banks, the hypothetical language, the machines that threatened to master men, as in the war of 1914-1918 and in the industrial system of to-day they have mastered men and made them their slaves. There was a youthful vigor in "Erewhon," a joyous negligence as to where the blow should fall, a sense of not being responsible for the world the author flicked with his lash, which saved the book from the condemnation that would have been its fate had the Victorians taken it seriously. It was an uneven book, beginning with vivid narrative in the best tradition of Defoe, losing itself finally in difficult argument, and cut short in mid-career.

"Erewhon Revisited" is much better constructed.

The old craftsman has profited by his years of labor in the British Museum. He has a story to tell, and tells it, weighting it with satire judiciously, as a fisherman weights his set line. If his tale becomes unreal it is only when he knows the author is ready to hear the author in person. If the Erewhon of his first visit does not fit his new conception he ruthlessly changes it. One misses the satiric *tours de force* of the first "Erewhon." There is nothing so brilliant as the chapters on disease and machines which for fifty years since life has been illustrating. But "Erewhon Revisited" is a finished book; it has artistic unity.

And why does Butler revisit Erewhon? Not because he was trained as a priest and must have an excuse to rediscuss theology, although the story of the book suggests this explanation. Higgs, the mysterious stranger of "Erewhon," who escaped by a balloon, has become a subject for myth. In Erewhon he is declared the child of the sun. Miracles gather about the supreme miracle of his air-born departure. His "Sayings," a mixture of Biblical quotation and homely philosophy, strained through Erewhonian intellects, become a new ethics and a new theology. His clothes are adopted for national wear (although through uncertainty as to how to put them on one part of the kingdom goes with buttons and pockets behind). Sunchildism becomes the state religion. The musical banks, which had been trading in stale idealism, take it over and get new life; and the professors of Bridgeford, the intellectuals of the kingdom, capitalize it, as we say to-day, and thus tighten their grip on the public's mind and purse.

Butler's purpose is transparent. It is not, as Longmans, who refused the work, believed, to attack Christianity. It is rather to expose the ease with which a good man and his message (Higgs brought with him to Erewhon evangelical Christianity) can become miraculous, can become an instrument for politics and a cause of sham. Indeed, Butler says in so many words to the Anglicans of his day: "Hold fast to your Christianity, for false as it is it is better than what its enemies would substitute; but go easy with the miraculous, the mythical, the ritualistic. These 'tamper with the one sure and everlasting word of God revealed to us by human experience.' "

All this is permanent enough, but I cannot believe, as most commentators do, that it is the heart of the book; or if it is the heart of the book, it is not its fire. The satiric rage of Butler, who in the person of Higgs returns to Erewhon to find himself deified, does not fall upon the fanatic worshipers of the sunchild, nor even upon the musical banks who have grown strong through his cult. It kindles for the ridiculous Hanky and Panky, professors respectively of worldly wisdom and worldly unwisdom at Bridgeford, and hence, according to Mr. Acklom, the antipathy toward Butler of all college professors.

But it is not because they are professors that Butler hates Hanky and Panky; it is because they represent that guaranteed authority which in every civilization

can and does exploit the passions and the weaknesses
of human nature for its own material welfare. Butler
had been conducting a lifelong warfare against
scholars who defended the *status quo* of the church
and against scientists who were consolidating a
strategic (and remunerative) position for themselves
in the universities. He saw, or thought he saw, English religion milked for the benefit of Oxford and Cambridge graduates needful of "livings"; and Darwinism
and the new sciences generally being swept into the
maw of the same professionally intellectual class. A
free lance himself, with a table in the British Museum,
some books and a deficit instead of an income from his
intellectual labors, he attacked the vested interests of
his world.

He exposed the dangers which wait upon all miraculous religions, the shams which they give birth to. But
not because he was obsessed with theology. If he
had lived in the nineteen hundreds he would have
studied, I think, sociology and economics instead of
theology and biology. He would have attacked, in
England, the House of Lords instead of Oxford, and
had an eye for the intellectuals who are beginning to
sway the mighty power of the labor unions. He would
have been a Radical-Conservative and voted against
both the British Labor party and the Coalition. In
America he would have lashed the trusts, execrated the
Anti-Saloon League, admired and been exasperated by
Mr. Wilson, hated the Republican party, and probably
have voted for it lest worse follow its defeat. He would

have been, in short, a liberal of a species very much needed just now in America, a bad party man, destructive rather than constructive, no leader, but a satirist when, God knows, we need one for the clearing of our mental atmosphere.

And unless I am wrong throughout this brief analysis, Samuel Butler, who mentally and spiritually is essentially our contemporary, would not, if he were writing now, concern himself with theology at all, but with the shams and unreasons which are the vested tyrannies set over us to-day. Erewhon, when we last hear of it, is about to become a modern colonial state. Its concern is with an army and with economics. Chow-Bok, the savage, now become a missionary bishop, is about to administer its ecclesiastical system. Its spiritual problems no longer center upon the validity of miraculous tradition and the logic of a theological code. But the vested interests (represented by Pocus, the son of Hanky) remain. These Butler would attack in the needed fashion. These remain the enemy.

VII
Conclusion

Defining the Indefinable

I AM well aware that literature or even such an inconsiderable part of literature as this gay book on my desk or the poem on the printed page, as a whole is indefinable. Every critic of literature from Aristotle down has let some of it slip between his fingers. If he describes the cunning form of a play or a story, then the passion in it, or the mood behind it, eludes him. If he defines the personality of the writer, the art which makes all the difference between feeling and expression escapes definition. No ten philosophers yet agree as to whether beauty is an absolute quality, or simply an attribute of form, whether a poem is beautiful because it suggests and approaches an archetype, or whether it is beautiful because it perfectly expresses its subject.

And yet when the ambition to explain and describe and define everything is humbly set aside there remains a good honest job for the maker of definitions, and it is a job that can be done. I may not be able to tell what art is, but I can tell what it isn't. I may fail to make a formula for literature, but I can try at least to tell what Thomas Hardy has chiefly accomplished, define Conrad's essential quality, point out the nature of romantic naturalism, and distinguish between sentiment and sentimentality. And if such things were ever worth doing they are worth doing now.

Only a prophet dares say that we are at the beginning of a great creative period in the United States, but any open-eyed observer can see that an era of American literary criticism is well under way. The war, which confused and afterward dulled our thinking, stirred innumerable critical impulses, which are coming to the surface, some like bubbles and others like boils, but some as new creations of the American intellect. The new generation has shown itself acrimoniously critical. It slaps tradition and names its novels and poetry as Adam named the animals in the garden, out of its own imagination. The war shook it loose from convention, and like a boy sent away to college, its first impulse is to disown the Main Street that bore it. Youth of the 90's admired its elders and imitated them unsuccessfully. Youth of the nineteen twenties imitates France and Russia of the 70's, and contemporary England. It may eventually do more than the 90's did with America; in the meantime, while it flounders in the attempt to create, it is at least highly critical. Furthermore, the social unrest, beginning before the war and likely to outlast our time, has made us all more critical of literature. Mark Twain's "Yankee in King Arthur's Court" turned the milk of Tennyson's aristocratic "Idylls" sour. The deep drawn undercurrent of socialistic thinking urges us toward a new consideration of all earlier writing, to see what may be its social significance. The "churl," the "hind," the "peasant," the "first servant" and "second country-man," who were the mere transitions of earlier stories now are central in literature. They come with a challenge, and when we read Galsworthy, Wells, Sinclair, Dreiser, Hardy's "The Dynasts," Bennett—we are conscious of criticizing life as we read. The pale cast of thought has sicklied modern pages. The more serious works of art are also literary criticism.

Again, there is the mingling of the peoples, greatest of course in America. Our aliens used to be subservient to the national tradition. They went about becoming rich Americans and regarded the Anglo-American culture as a natural phenomenon, like the climate, to which after a while they would accustom themselves. Their children were born in it. But now it is different. The Jews particularly, who keep an Oriental insistence upon logic even longer than a racial appearance, have passed the acquisitive stage and begin to throw off numerous intellectuals, as much at home in English as their fellow Americans, but critical of the American emotions, and the American way of thinking, as only a brain formed by different traditions can be. Soon the Mediterranean races domiciled here will pass into literary expressiveness. It is as impossible that we should not have criticism of the national tradition expressed in our literature as that an international congress should agree upon questions of ethics or religion.

And of course the new internationalism, which is far more vigorous than appears on the surface, favors such criticism. The war brought America and Europe two thousand miles closer, and the habit of interest in what Europeans are thinking, once acquired, is not likely to be lost. No American writer of promise can hope now to escape comparison with the literatures of Western Europe, and comparison means a new impulse to criticism.

Fundamental, creative criticism — like Sainte-Beuve's, Matthew Arnold's, Walter Pater's, like Dryden's, Brunetière's, De Gourmont's, or Croce's—will presumably come. The conditions, both of publication and of audience, are ripe for it now in the United States. But there is a good deal of spade work in the study of literature to be done first, and still more education of the reading American mind. One reason why Lowell was not a great critic was because his scholarship was defective, or, to put it more fairly, because the scholarship of his contemporaries, with whose knowledge he might have buttressed his own, was incomplete. And if a twentieth century Sainte-Beuve should begin to write for general American readers, it is doubtful whether they would accept his premises. Says the intellectual, why *should* he write for the general public? I answer that if he writes for coteries only, if he is disdainful of the intelligent multitude, he will never understand *them*, and so will not comprehend the national literature which it is his function to stimulate, interpret, and guide.

The spade work of criticism is research, investigation into the facts of literature and into its social background. The scholar is sometimes, but not often, a critic. He finds out what happened, and often why it happened. He analyzes, but he does not usually make a synthesis. He writes history, but he cannot prophesy, and criticism is prophecy implied or direct. Few outside the universities realize the magnitude of American research into literature, even into American literature, which has been relatively neglected. A thousand spades have been at work for a generation. We are getting the facts, or we are learning how to get them.

But before we may expect great criticism we must educate our public, and ourselves, in that clear vision of what is and what is not, which from Aristotle down has been the preliminary to criticism. A humble, but a useful, way to begin is by definition.

I use definition in no pedantic sense. I mean, in general, logical definition where the class or *genus* of the thing to be described—whether best-selling novel or sentimental tendency—is first made clear, and then its *differentia*, its differences from the type analyzed out and assorted. But this process in literature cannot be as formal as logic. Good literature cannot be bound by formulas. Yet when a poem charged with hot emotion, or a story that strays into new margins of experience, is caught and held until one can compare it with others, see the curve on which it is moving, guess its origin and its aim, forever after it becomes easier to understand, more capable of being thought about and appreciated. And when the current of taste of some new generation that overflows conventions and washes forward, or backward, into regions long unlaved, is viewed as a current, its direction plotted, its force estimated, its quality compared, why that is definition, and some good will come of it.

Some general definition of that intellectual emotion which we call good reading is especially needed in America. Most of us, if we are native born, have been educated by a set of literary conventions arranged in convenient categories. That is more or less true of all literary education, but it is particularly true in the United States, where the formal teaching of English literature *per se* began, where, as nowhere else in the world, there was a great and growing population eager to become literate and with no literary traditions behind it. The student from a bookless home learned to think of his literature as primarily something to be studied; the teacher who had to teach thousands like him was forced to reduce living literature to dead categories in order that a little of it at least should be taught. Thousands of Americans, therefore, of our generation emerged from their training with a set of literary definitions which they assumed to be true and ‚supposed to be culture. Only true definitions of what literature really is can break up such fossilized defining.

On the other hand, that large proportion of our best reading population which is not native in its traditions offers a different but equally important problem. How can the son of a Russian Jew, whose father lived in a Russian town, who himself has been brought up in clamorous New York, understand Thoreau, let us say, or John Muir, or Burroughs, or Willa Cather, without some defining of the nature of the American environment and the relation between thought and the soil? How is an intelligent German-American, whose cultural tradition has been thoroughly Teutonic, to make himself at home in a literature whose general character, like its language, is English, without some defining of the Anglo-American tradition? Lincoln must be defined for him; Milton must be defined for him; most of all perhaps Franklin must be defined for him. I have chosen elementary examples, but my meaning should be sufficiently clear.

And the American critic—by which I mean you, O discriminating reader, as well as the professional who puts pen to paper—is equally in need of the art of definition. The books we read and write are on different planes of absolute excellence or unworthiness. There is—to take the novel—the story well calculated to pass a pleasant hour but able to pass nothing else; there is the story with a good idea in it and worth reading for the idea only; there is the story worthless as art but usefully catching some current phase of experience; and there is the fine novel which will stand any test for insight, skill, and truth. Now it is folly to apply a single standard to all these types of story. It can be done, naturally, but it accomplishes nothing except to eliminate all but the shining best. That is a task for history. In the year in which we live—and it is sometimes necessary to remind the austerer critic that we always live in the present—there are a hundred books, of poetry, of essays, of biography, of fiction, which are by no means of the first rank and yet are highly important, if only as news of what the world, in our present, is thinking and feeling. They cannot be judged, all of them, on the top plane of perfect excellence; and if we judge them all on any other plane, good, better, best get inextricably mixed.

For example, consider once more a novel which at the moment of this writing is a best-seller, and which with reference to its popularity I have discussed in an earlier essay. I mean Mr. Hutchinson's "If Winter Comes." This book is essentially the tragedy of a good and honest soul thrown by harsh circumstance into an environment which is bound to crush him. He has the wrong wife, he has the wrong business associates, the girl he loves is separated from him by moral barriers. If he breaks through these he injures irreparably his own sense of what is due to his God and his fellow man. His instincts of charity, humor, and love rebound upon him. He is too Christian for England, and too guileless for life. This is a worthy theme, and yet if we judge this novel on the highest plane it fails miserably. For Mr. Hutchinson stacks the cards. He gives his hero his way and his salvation, after much suffering, by a series of lucky accidents. He destroys the problem he creates, by forging an answer.

But this novel should not be finally judged on the

highest plane. It is not a tragedy, it is a romance. It belongs on the plane below, the plane of stories told to meet the secret desires of humanity, which have little to do with reality, and are quite oblivious to fact. On this plane "If Winter Comes" ranks highly, for it is poignantly told, there is life in its characters, and truth in the best of its scenes. Definition saves us from calling a good novel great; it spares us the unnecessary error of calling a good and readable story bad because it is not a triumph of consistent art.

It is hard enough in all conscience to see that a given book is good for *this* but not good for *that;* may be praised for its plot, but certainly has not character enough to get long life. But when the difficulty of adjusting standards is increased by the irresponsible hullabaloo of commercial appreciation, no wonder that sensible people estimate foolishly, and critics of standing are induced to write for publication remarks that some day will (or should) make them sick. For the publishers' "blurb" confuses all standards. Every book is superlative in everything. And the hack reviewer, when he likes a book, likes everything and applies Shakespearian adjectives and Tolstoyan attributes to creatures of dust and tinsel, or blunders helplessly into dispraise of scholarship, restraint, subtlety, taste, originality—anything that he does not understand.

There is no help except to set books upon their planes and assort them into their categories—which is merely to define them before beginning to criticize. This is elementary work as I have said, which may lead the critic only so far as the threshold, and cannot always give the reader that complete and sympathetic comprehension of what he has read which is the final object of literary criticism. However, in an age when over-emphasis has been commercialized, and where the powerful forces of print can be mobilized and sent charging everywhere to bowl down contrary opinions, it is indispensable.

Scholarly books have been dispraised because they were not exciting; fine novels have been sneered at because they were hard to read; cheap stories have been proclaimed great because they wore a pretense of seriousness; sentimentality has been welcomed because it was warm hearted; indecency has been condemned for immorality; immorality has slipped through as romance; daring has been mistaken for novelty; painstaking dulness, for careful art; self-revelation, for world knowledge; pretty writing, for literature; violence, for strength; and warped and unhealthy egoism for the wise sincerity which is the soul of literature. In all such instances definition is the prophylactic, and often the cure.

Writers, most of all, need to define their tasks. I do not mean their technical problems merely, although I cannot conceive that a dramatist or playwright, who has his subject well in mind, can possibly be hurt by thinking out his methods with the most scrupulous care. Lubbock's recent book on "The Craft of Fiction" has emphasized an art of approach and point of view in the great novelists which was thoroughly conscious, even though they may never have tried to formulate it in words. I mean particularly the defining of their themes, their objectives. Many modern novels of the better class, and a great many modern poems, seem to me awash and wallowing like derelicts on the high seas. They are successful enough in this, excellent in that, but they get nowhere, because the writers had felt the emotion that made them, or suffered the experience, but never defined it in terms of all emotion, all experience, never considered its end. The three dots . . . of modern literature are significant. We break off our efforts, partly no doubt because we seek effects of impressionism, more often because imagination went no further. Near things are sharp and expressed with remarkable vividness, ultimate objectives are blurred, which is to say, they lack definition.

May the shades of Dr. Johnson, Charles Lamb, Emerson, and all great individualists protect us from bad definitions, and especially from rigid or formal ones! Bad definitions destroy themselves, for if they are thoroughly bad no one believes them, and if they contain those pleasing half truths which a generation loves to suckle upon, why then after their vogue they will wither into nothingness. Such definitions are of the letter, and die by it, but stiff, clumsy definitions kill the spirit. To define a great man by a rigid formula is to sink to the lowest practice of the worst class rooms. To define a tendency so sharply that it cannot flow without breaking the definition, is a lecturer's trick for which audiences should stone him. Solemn generalizations which squat upon a book like an ostrich on a goose egg and hatch out vast moral philosophies are to be dreaded like the devil, as are, equally, the critics with pet theories, who, having defined them, make everything from a squib to an epic fit their definition.

Definitions which classify without margins are a special evil: the division into literature and journalism for example, with no allowance for interlocking; or the confident separation of all books into categories of good or bad. Wholesale definitions are also objectionable, where having defined a poem as magazine verse, or a collection of articles as a magazine, or a book as a sex story, or a man as a journalist, or a tendency as erratic or erotic, you think you have said something. May the muse of clear thinking, and the little humorous gods who keep the sense of proportion balancing, protect us from these also.

It occurs to me that I have made but a lame attempt to define definition. This, however, is as it should be. For definition, in the sense in which I am using it, like literature, has much of the indefinable. It is a tool merely, or better still, because broader, a device by which the things we enjoy and that profit us may be placed in perspective, ranged, compared, sorted, and distinguished. It is what Arnold meant by seeing steadily and seeing whole. It is the scientist's microscope that defines relationship, and equally the painter's brush that by a touch reveals the hidden shapes of nature and the blend of colors. It is, like these instruments, a *means* and not an *end*. May pedants, scholiasters, formalists, and dilettantes take to heart this final description of literary definition!

Quite unconsciously for the most part, but occasionally with purpose aforethought, the essays in this book have been written as literary definitions. Its unity lies in the attempt, which at least has been sincere, to grasp, turn, study in a serious, humorous, ironical, anything but a flippant mood, the living forms of literature as they have risen into consciousness and challenged definition.

THE END